THE Sardinian COOKBOOK

THE Sardinian COOKBOOK

The Cooking and Culture of a Mediterranean Island

Viktorija Todorovska

AN AGATE IMPRINT

CHICAGO

Copyright © 2013 Viktorija Todorovska

All rights reserved. No part of this book may be reproduced or transmitted in any form or by any means, electronic or mechanical, including photocopying, recording, or by any information storage and retrieval system, without express written permission from the publisher.

Printed in Korea.

All photographs copyright © 2013 Viktorija Todorovska and Michael Potts

Design by Brandtner Design.

Library of Congress Cataloging-in-Publication Data

Todorovska, Viktorija, 1971-
  The Sardinian Cookbook : The Cooking and Culture of a Unique Mediterranean Island / by Viktorija Todorovska.
     pages cm
  Summary: "Recipes from the Italian island of Sardinia, with information about Sardinian culture, history, geography, and cuisine. Includes photographs"--Provided by publisher.
  Includes index.
  ISBN-13: 978-1-57284-147-5 (flexibound)
  ISBN-10: 1-57284-147-8 (flexibound)
  ISBN-13: 978-1-57284-730-9 (ebook)
  ISBN-10: 1-57284-730-1 (ebook)
  1. Cooking, Italian. 2. Cooking--Italy--Sardinia. 3. Food habits--Italy--Sardinia. 4. Sardinia (Italy)--Description and travel. 5. Sardinia (Italy)--Social life and customs. I. Title.
  TX723.T625 2013
  641.5945'9--dc23
                      2013016266

13 14 15 16   10 9 8 7 6 5 4 3 2 1

Surrey Books is an imprint of Agate Publishing. Agate books are available in bulk at discount prices. For more information, go to agatepublishing.com.

To my Sardinian friends: Both those I know and those I am yet to meet

Table of Contents

FOREWORD 12

INTRODUCTION 14

BEAUTIFUL SARDINIA 16

Geography and Nature 21
    Nuraghi 27
    Invasions and Conquests: "He Who Comes from the Sea, Comes to Rob" 28
    Sardinian Language (Sardo) 29
    Murales 30

Sardinian Food 31
    Foods of the Interior 32
    The Sea and Its Bounty 35
    Food as Tradition 36
    Bread 39
    Cheese 41

Sardinian Ingredients 45
    Bottarga 45
    Extra Virgin Olive Oil 46
    Honey 46
    Saffron 47
    Sundried Tomatoes 47

Wine 49
    Liqueurs 53

ANTIPASTI 54
    Artichokes with Bottarga 56
    Burrida, *Cagliari-Style* 57

Burrida, *Oristano-Style* 58
Deviled Eggs 59
Focaccia Sarda 60
Fresh Fava with Mint 63
Herbed Breadcrumbs 64
Homemade Breadcrumbs 65
Marinated Olives 65
Mini Meatballs 66
Mullet Bottarga 68
Octopus in Tomato and Garlic Sauce (Agliata) 69
Octopus with Celery 71
Pane Carasau *with Pecorino* 73
Pane Carasau *with Olive Oil and Sea Salt* (Pane Guttiau) 74
Raw, Fresh Fava with Olive Oil 76
Shrimp Salad 77
Steamed Mussels 79
Sweet Pea Frittata 80
Tomato Bruschetta with Bottarga 81
Vegetable Fritters 82
Vegetable Panada 84

PRIMI 86

Pasta and Risotto 88

Baked Fregola *with Pecorino* 90
Baked Semolina Gnocchi with Meat Sauce 92
Corkscrew-Shaped Pasta with Zucchini Cream and Bottarga 94
Couscous with Vegetables 96
Fettuccine with Olives, Capers, and Tuna 99

Fregola *with Clams* 101
Fregola *with Sausage and Pecorino* 102
Lasagne with Tuna and Pesto 104
Linguine with Lobster 106
Lorighitas with Free-Range Chicken Sauce 108
Malloreddus (Gnocchetti Sardi) 110
Malloreddus *with Fresh Fava and Pecorino* 113
Malloreddus *with Meat Sauce* 114
Malloreddus *with Young Pecorino* 115
Malloreddus alla Campidanese (with Sausage) 116
Pane Frattau 118
Penne with Wild Fennel and Pancetta 121
Potato and Mint Ravioli 122
Potato and Mint Ravioli in Tomato Sauce 124
Potato and Mint Ravioli with Lamb Ragù 125
Ricotta and Greens Ravioli 126
Ricotta and Greens Ravioli with Wild Fennel 128
Ravioli with Eggplant and Sausage 130
Rigatoni with Wild Boar Sauce 131
Risotto with Bottarga *(Mullet Roe)* 133
Risotto with Wild Asparagus 135
Seafood Pasta 137
Spaghetti with Bottarga 138
Spaghetti with Clams 141
Spaghetti with Crushed Red Pepper 142
Spaghetti with Tuna and Olives 144
Spaghetti with Wild Asparagus 147
Spaghetti with Zucchini and Vernaccia di Oristano 148
Tagliatelle with Walnuts 149

Soups **151**
   Artichoke Heart Soup 152
   Asparagus Soup 154
   Bean Soup 156
   Bean and Cabbage Soup 157
   Beet Green and Fregola *Soup* (Lampazu) 158
   Fava and Pork Stew (Favata) 160
   Fennel Soup 161
   Fregola *in Cheese Broth* (Fregola in Brodo) 163
   Garbanzo Bean Soup with Wild Fennel 164
   Lentil Soup with Potatoes and Beets 167
   Minestrone with Fava 168
   Minestrone with Garbanzo Beans 171
   Pea Soup with Pasta and Ricotta 173
   Seafood Soup 174
   Zucchini Soup with Fregola 177
   Zuppa Gallurese (Zuppa Quatta) 178

SECONDI **179**

Seafood **180**
   Baccalà *with Tomatoes, Olives, and Wild Fennel* 181
   Calamari Stew 182
   Fish in Salt Crust 184
   Grilled Sardines 185
   Octopus, Potato, and Green Bean Salad 187
   Mussels in Spicy Tomato Sauce 188
   Sardines with Lemon, Garlic, and Parsley 189
   Sea Bream with Red Onion 190
   Striped Bass with Vegetables 191
   Swordfish with Peas 192

Poultry **193**
    Braised Chicken with Myrtle and Red Wine 194
    Chicken with Capers 195
    Chicken with Tomatoes and Olives 196
    Chicken with Vernaccia di Oristano 197

Meats **199**
    Sanguinaccio *(Blood Sausage)* 200
    Goat with Wild Fennel 201
    Cordula 202
    Lamb Stew 205
    Lamb with Fennel and Sundried Tomatoes 206
    Lamb Stew with Potatoes 207
    Meatballs 208
    Panadas 211
    Pork Chops with Olives and Vernaccia di Oristano 213
    Pork Roast with Mediterranean Herbs 214
    Spring Lamb with Artichokes 215
    Spring Lamb with Fava 217
    Tripe Sardinian-Style 218
    Veal Meatballs 220
    Veal Porterhouse Steaks with Vernaccia di Oristano 221
    Wild Boar in Red Wine 222
    Wild Boar in Sweet and Sour Sauce 225

CONTORNI **226**
    Baked Artichoke Hearts with Cheese 227
    Baked Eggplant 228
    Endive with Extra Virgin Olive Oil 229

Fava	231
Fava Salad	232
Fava with Pancetta	233
Potatoes and Artichokes	235
Potatoes with Fennel and Capers	236
Potatoes with Mediterranean Herbs	237
Roasted Tomatoes	238
Sautéed Zucchini	239
Zucchini Salad with Tomatoes and Cheese	240

DOLCI — 243

Almond and Orange Brittle (Aranzada)	244
Amarettus (Amaretti)	246
Butter Cookies	247
Chocolate Mirto *Truffles*	248
Crema Catalana	250
Fig Tart with Sapa	251
Pardulas	252
Pecorino with Honey	254
Raisin Cookies (Pabassinos *or* Papassinus)	255
Ricotta Cake	257
Sebadas *(or* Seadas*)*	258

SOURCES — 260

ACKNOWLEDGMENTS — 261

INDEX — 264

ABOUT THE AUTHOR — 271

Foreword

Well before we opened our restaurant, A16, I began my Italian love affair on the island of Sardinia. Its beauty is renowned, but the elongated island is also a sanctuary for ampelographers (botanists who specialize in grapevines), foodies, anthropologists, and vacationers. Sardinia's west coast is world renowned for *bottarga* (the pressed, dried roe of tuna or gray mullet), equestrians, and Spanish colonial cities like Alghero that reflect the diverse lifestyle of the island. During the summer months, flights to the island are jammed with Italian sun worshippers seeking natural beauty, celebratory evenings, and *la dolce vita* at its finest.

Vermentino di Gallura was the first Sardinian wine I'd ever tried, and it's still a favorite. This stone-fruit, mineral-tinged dry wine never fails to amaze me with how beautifully it matches the vast array of seafood and tangy pecorinos found on the island that can't be missed. It can be found in the U.S. as well. The white grape nuragus, which is even more widely planted than the popular vermentino, is named after the prehistoric people who were indigenous to the island. The hard-to-find Passito, which comes from the nasco grape found inland near the port of Karalis, is a rare treat that offers up yet another story of ancient Sardinia with its musk, orange rind, and almond flavors. The white wines of Sardinia draw one in and romanticize the island's ability to take over the senses and allow time to slow down with the ebb and flow of the surrounding sea, in welcome contrast to the briskness of modernity. That is *Sardegna*.

Sardinia's red wines take you into the heart of the island, capturing sun-ripened flavors that showcase the wild mountain underbrush, myrtle, orange rinds, and medjool dates. I look for these unique flavors in reds such as Cannonau, Carignano del Sulcis, Covale, and Cagnulari. The reds have varying bodyweights depending on what part of the island and style of producer you discover. The lighter reds from Alghero can easily pair with a local fisherman's stew or *fregola* dish, whereas the Carignano del Sulcis, which hails from the southeast corner of Sardinia, pairs nicely with lamb or suckling pork. I also love the way the reds' sweeter tannins pair with bitter greens and earthy spices.

For centuries, *Sardos* have steeled themselves against coastal invasions, resiliently preserving the island's perspective on life and culture, food, and wine. This also explains why, as a culture, they've also insulated themselves from the mainland. It's as if this sparsely populated island that seems to float, untethered, in the middle of the Mediterranean Sea has always wanted to be left alone. Its distance from Italy's west coast (111 miles eastward, across the Tyrrhenian Sea) also contributes to Sardinia seeming more foreign than any other region of the country. There's certainly something wild here, and not just in its prehistoric ruins or aggressive driving styles (some refer to Sardinia's *strada statale* that connects Calgiari with Porto Torres as "Italy's most dangerous highway"). Its arid terrain includes desolate, brush-filled inland stretches and striking coastlines. The air alternates from piercing sirocco winds from northern Africa to tranquil sea breezes. The combination stirs something inside the casual visitor.

—Shelley Lindgren
Owner and Wine Director, A16, San Francisco, California

Introduction

The moment I learned how to say "ciao," I embarked on a lifelong love affair with Italy and its unforgettable foods and wines. I am not Italian by birth, but I am Italian at heart. Utterly passionate about Italy and all things Italian, I continue to explore every corner of this enchanting land and soak up the knowledge of generations of cooks and food lovers. I didn't have an Italian grandmother of my own to cook with, but in my travels I have been adopted by many grandmothers and aunts who graciously taught me their secrets and showed me dishes that inspire love and passion.

Being an outsider has advantages: I can approach the foods and wines of Italy from a unique perspective and explain them to others along with the cultural context necessary for better understanding. Outsiders notice things natives take for granted.

As an outsider, I am enchanted by every new dish and every fresh ingredient; every variation of a recipe makes me want to know the reasons for it. I study the history and meaning of Italian foods so I can better explain them. I look beyond the familiar and find new things to be excited about around every corner.

In my explorations of the delicious, I have been drawn to lesser known regions—parts of Italy that have been overlooked in the past by cookbook writers, chefs, and travelers. I love the thrill of traveling to areas few have visited, villages that quietly and proudly carry on traditions few are aware of. I love telling the inspiring stories of these places and people, stories full of passion, dedication, and love of tradition.

"Why Sardinia?" I often heard from others while I was working on this book. The simple answer is that I have been fascinated with Sardinia for a long time. In 1995, a bus driver in Tuscany asked me if I was Sardinian. The question made me beam with pride. As time went on, I was asked the same question again and again, and I was always flattered. I am not sure it was always meant as a compliment—after all, many Italians see Sardinia as a world unto itself, an isolated and unfamiliar place—but I took it as such. I was proud to be considered Sardinian even before I visited the majestic island. All the Sardinians I had ever met, after all, were impressive people: kind, generous, proud of their island, and always eager to share its stories and traditions.

Over the years, Sardinia stayed on my mind. When I tasted my first *sebada* in a class at Apicius, a cooking school in Florence, I wondered how this treat came to be. Who came up with the brilliant idea to stuff dough with fresh, soft cheese, fry it to a crisp, and drizzle bitter honey on it? A genius, I decided. And thus my desire to see Sardinia and taste more of her pleasures grew.

When I finally visited Sardinia, I found countless fascinating traditions, tantalizing flavors, unexpected combinations, and never-before-seen dishes. They fueled my desire to get to know the island and its people. On return trips, I delved deeper into the island's history, traditions, and unique foods. The more I learned, the more I wanted to know—because it is difficult to say that you truly know Sardinia. Around every corner, in every kitchen imprinted with the cooking of generations, there lies a new story, a new recipe, a new treasure to be discovered. So, my pursuit of the delicious continues.

In this book, I have gathered traditional Sardinian recipes that were generously shared with me by cooks of all ages—both professionals and home cooks who have lovingly fed their families and friends for years. Sardinians opened their homes and hearts to me and treated me to unforgettable experiences every culinary explorer longs for. This book is dedicated to them. I hope I can do them, and their island, justice.

Beautiful Sardinia

A rugged interior, a breathtaking coastline, centuries-old traditions, and proud people in love with their land: This is Sardinia, the second largest island in the Mediterranean and one of the oldest lands in Europe. Today, Sardinia is part of Italy. But the many invasions it saw over the centuries left a strong mark on the island's culture, creating a fascinating blend of Spanish, French, and Italian influences—and a dash of Moorish. It is rightfully described as the least Italian of all Italian regions, but that description doesn't do it justice. Sardinia is Sardinia, and everything on the island speaks to that. From

its jetsetting Emerald Coast (*Costa Smeralda*) in the northeast to the rugged interior, each piece of this enchanting land is different and tells stories of conquest, perseverance, and pride.

Slightly closer to Tunisia than to Italy, Sardinia is the essence of the Mediterranean: sunny and green year-round under a blanket of fragrant Mediterranean brush. Most visitors come to Sardinia for its breathtaking coast and emerald sea. But seeing only the coast means missing the real Sardinia—the Sardinia of proud and generous people, the Sardinia of folklore, traditions, and a way of life that seems to have disappeared from other parts of Italy.

Islands are always unique, as if the water that separates them from the mainland with which they are politically connected is an insurmountable barrier. Sardinia abounds in that island mystique, that charm you cannot easily describe. This faraway land enveloped in mystery owes its character to the distances that separate it from the mainland.

Isolated, enigmatic, and intriguing, Sardinia, with its history of dominations and conquests, has managed to preserve its unique character. Its culture has incorporated various influences, but hasn't lost its Sardinian-ness.

Sardinia is distinguished not only because other Italians see it as different, but also because Sardinians themselves see their island as different from all other lands. Its landscape of silences, sunshine, rugged mountains, mysterious caves, and splendid waterfalls is framed by a culture of pride and passion about everything Sardinian. And this makes Sardinia matchless. It is not just a land: It is a character with a personality and a spirit, a soul that demands to be appreciated.

D.H. Lawrence depicted Sardinia as "lost between Europe and Africa and belonging to nowhere. Belonging to nowhere, never having belonged to anywhere." He was right in that it is impossible to compare

Sardinia to other Italian regions or Mediterranean islands. It is like no other place. Arrive with an open mind and an open heart, and immerse yourself in the singular experience that is Sardinia.

Geography and Nature

Sardinia is the second largest island in the Mediterranean, only slightly smaller than Sicily. But it is home to only about 1.6 million people—significantly fewer than Sicily. It is the farthest island from the Italian mainland. Corsica, a French island, is several miles to the north, so standing on the northern coast of Sardinia you feel like you can touch France.

Sardinia's landscape is unpredictable: desert dunes, snow-capped mountains, lagoons full of flamingoes, freshwater lakes, extinct vol-

canoes, and underground caves give the island a distinct beauty. One Sardinian legend says that after God created the Earth, he collected the leftover pieces, threw them together, and stepped on them. And Sardinia was born!

Sardinia has over 1,800 kilometers of coastline, almost a quarter of the entire coast of Italy. From the powdery white sand of the beaches to the promontories and deep bays, the coast dazzles with beauty and variety. It is also one of the most pristine coasts in Europe, the sea always limpid, clear, and emerald in color. The *Costa Smeralda*, which is considered one of the most beautiful coastlines in all of Europe, attracts millions of tourists every year. Further south on the east side of the island, the coast becomes rugged and inaccessible, with steep cliffs dropping almost vertically into the sea. The sand dunes of the west coast are so different from the landscape of the east coast that it's difficult to believe they are only 100 or so miles away. On the south and west coasts are some of Sardinia's most beautiful beaches, as well as some of her most important ports. These ports served as places of call for invaders going all the way back to the Phoenicians.

But the coast is only a fraction of this beautiful island. In the past, when the coast was the entry point for invasions, the local population lived mostly in the interior. Here, most of Sardinia's traditions were

born and continue to flourish. The landscape of the interior is mysterious and ever changing. In the region of Gallura in the northeast, outcrops of granite dot the landscape as if the land shifted only yesterday, pushing the rocks to the surface through the green carpet of thyme, rosemary, myrtle, and heather.

Further south, the high hills of Supramonte di Orgosolo and Barbagia form the true interior of the island. In many ways, this is the heart of Sardinia, the cradle of its most prominent traditions. The ruggedness of Barbagia made it inaccessible to many invaders, so its population lived in relative isolation for centuries. It was the Romans who, unable to conquer this hilly region, named it "barbarie," after what they considered to be the barbarian ferocity of its people. The name remains to this day.

Barbagia's geographic isolation is responsible for its unique history and way of life. Over time, customs, foods, and traditions emerged in the region, increasing the feeling of differentness among those who lived there. To this day, it remains one of the more difficult regions of Sardinia to get to know. As Sardinian journalist and author Michela Murgia once wrote, "going to Barbagia is different from getting into Barbagia."

But getting to know Barbagia is absolutely worthwhile. Each town in this rugged heart of Sardinia has distinctive customs and history. The people in each village speak a different dialect, even if only several

miles separate them from neighboring villages. Each town showcases different types of art, from the *murales* (murals) of Orgosolo to the masks of Mamoiada.

South of mysterious Barbagia lies the only real mountain on the island: Gennargentu, an ancient and rugged massif. It is not very high, but it is nevertheless impressive. Its name means "wind gate," as the mountain's shape creates wind currents. Its deep canyons and hidden caves alternate with oak forests and Mediterranean brush, giving the area a matchless beauty and mystique.

To the west, the hills and mountains give way to the fertile Campidano plain, which stretches from Cagliari in the south to Oristano on the west coast. Cultivated since Roman times, the Campidano was the main source of grain for the Roman Empire. Today, vines, olives, and almonds thrive here, and sheep graze peacefully on rich pasture land.

The southwest, which is rich in minerals, has long attracted foreigners. For centuries, they mined Sardinia's natural resources and sent them elsewhere. Abandoned mining towns stand witness to this dark chapter in Sardinian history—one of many chapters of conquests, suffering, and perseverance.

Everywhere you go in Sardinia, you are greeted with the kind of beauty that demands that you take notice. From flamingo-rich ponds in the west to breathtaking cliffs plunging into the Mediterranean in the east, from the vibrant capital of Cagliari and deserted mining towns in the south to Catalan-influenced Alghero in the north, Sardinia reveals her natural beauty slowly, one marvel at a time.

The plants that grow on Sardinia and the animals that roam its forests are also different from those on the mainland. Prickly green Mediterranean brush (*macchia*) covers the island, making it a vibrant green year-round. The brush's seductive, unmistakably Mediterranean aroma permeates Sardinian foods and wines, tugging at the heartstrings of Sardinians and seducing visitors.

Myrtle berries are used to make *mirto*, the island's famous *digestivo*, and their dried leaves flavor roasts and stews. Prickly pear, another fixture of the Sardinian landscape, is also used in cooking, especially in desserts and condiments. And *pompia*, a unique cross of several citrus fruits, is another tasty mystery waiting to be discovered. Flavorful onions, cardoons, tomatoes, peppers, and artichokes round out the ensemble of produce that gives Sardinian dishes unforgettable flavor.

It's not an exaggeration to describe Sardinia as a continent of its own, a place that gathers all that's most beautiful on Earth. Its natural beauty and individuality have outlasted many conquests and a turbulent history. Today, it continues to seduce curious travelers just as it did in the past.

NURAGHI

Sardinia has a long and fascinating history. In the Bronze Age, some 35 to 40 centuries ago, the island housed the Nuraghic people, one of the most advanced cultures in the Mediterranean. Even today, more than 7,000 stone towers (*nuraghi*) built by the Nuraghic people dot the island, making it an open-air museum.

These mysterious towers, which are a symbol of the island, are not found anywhere else in the Mediterranean, not even on the island of Corsica, which lies only a few miles away from the northern tip of Sardinia. The earliest of the *nuraghi* were single towers and formed a communication chain: another *nuraghi* could always be seen in the distance. Over time, the designs became more complex, with a central tower used as a watchtower and three or more peripheral ones. Today, the tallest of the nuraghi are monuments that can be visited with a guide, but many others are on private property. You see them everywhere, sheep peacefully grazing nearby as if it were the most natural thing to stand next to a stone structure over 30 centuries old.

INVASIONS AND CONQUESTS: "HE WHO COMES FROM THE SEA, COMES TO ROB"

Sardinia's strategic position, at the crossroads of the Mediterranean, has made it appealing to foreign powers throughout history. The island endured 1,500 years of conquests, occupations, and raids, all of which left a mark on the land and created a particular blend of cultures and influences.

The first outsiders to arrive were the Phoenicians, who landed on Sardinia's southwest coast around 1000 BC. They came in peace, seeking a place to rest and repair their ships while sailing between Tunisia and Spain. Attracted by Sardinia's natural resources, however, they advanced further inland and gradually expanded their settlements. But the native Sardi didn't sit idle: They rose to defend their island and defeated the Phoenician invaders.

Next came the Carthaginians, who expanded the old Phoenician settlements and moved further inland. As they did, they exploited the island's natural resources and enslaved the native Sardi. This is the beginning of Sardinia's history of conquest: The island, which had always been independent, became part of a larger colony.

Soon Rome rose to power, defeated Carthage, and colonized Sardinia. But the Romans never fully subdued the island. Years of rebellions and uprisings among the locals led to Barbagia's name. To this day, the ruins of Roman settlements serve as a reminder of the power of this ancient empire and its influence on Sardinia.

The fall of the Roman Empire paved the way for many other invasions: the Vandals, Byzantines, Arabs, and Spanish, to name a few. Even the maritime powers of Pisa and Genoa, which originally came to help free Sardinia of invaders, ended up staying and exploiting the island's rich natural resources.

Until it became part of unified Italy in 1861, Sardinia was ruled by foreign powers. Each left a mark, and this blend of influences has given the island a fascinating cultural and artistic heritage. Invaded in territory, but never conquered in spirit, Sardinia absorbed foreign influences but always stayed true to its traditions.

SARDINIAN LANGUAGE (SARDO)

Sardo, the native language of Sardinians, is linguistically recognized as a distinct language and not a dialect of Italian. Most linguists agree that of all Romance languages, Sardo is the closest to Latin. The variant of Sardo changes from village to village and town to town. Even villages several kilometers from each other use different words to express the same ideas.

Adding to this complexity is the fact that parts of the island speak a language completely distinct from Sardo. The language of Alghero is a medieval variant of Catalan; in the northeastern region of Gallura, the language is shaped by its proximity to Corsica and a long history of Corsican immigration; and in Carloforte on the island of San Pietro, the language is a blend of old-time Ligurian and North African. Perhaps this helps explain why many young Sardinians speak Italian instead of the language of their native town or village. The media broadcast mainly in Italian, and most Sardinian writers write in Italian. But in artistic forms of expression, such as rap, Sardo is still used to express protest and maintain a sense of individuality.

MURALES

The most visible artistic development of recent years are *murales* (murals), hundreds of which decorate the walls of Orgosolo and surrounding towns. *Murales* started appearing in 1975, to celebrate the thirtieth anniversary of the fall of fascism. They have spread to other towns on the island, but Orgosolo remains their spiritual home. They reflect the movement in Sardinian art toward depicting the island's national identity and social issues. Some *murales* depict images from history, including the workers' movement and the suffering of the local population, others reflect triumphs over foreign invaders and occupiers.

Sardinian Food

In Sardinia, food is family and community, togetherness and sharing. First-time visitors are often overwhelmed by Sardinian hospitality: From the moment you walk into someone's house, you become part of the family and will be treated to the best the host has to offer. It's useless to resist because the food keeps coming. And you'll leave with more food: homemade jam, salami, and the neighbor's cheese. Such a bounty of delectable foods might make you forget that for a long time, Sardinia was poor, and much of the population survived on one meal a day. But if you look more carefully, you will discover that this history of hard times is still clearly visible in Sardinia's food traditions. Poverty and isolation cultivated a cuisine based on local ingredients, with each dish deeply rooted in the geography and history of the region it came from.

For many centuries, the sea surrounding Sardinia inspired fear in Sardinians, who equated it with danger, foreign invaders, and malaria. The islanders lived in the inhospitable mountains of the interior, where no one unfamiliar with the terrain would dare venture. Thus, the traditional dishes of the island arise from shepherd and farming traditions, not from the sea—something that surprises many visitors.

The arrival of the Genoese in the thirteenth century introduced Sardinians to new foodways in the form of fish and shellfish. But to this day, only coastal cities have a strong tradition of seafood, and the dishes found there are always influenced by the foreigners who dominated them—Ligurians in the southwest and the north, and Spaniards on the west coast.

Sardinian cuisine is clearly divided into two parts: the cuisine of the sea and the cuisine of the land. Restaurant menus, especially those in more traveled areas, also reflect this division. Both cuisines are based on simple, local ingredients that give rise to extraordinary dishes—some of which cannot be found anywhere else. This use of local ingredients underscores the deep attachment Sardinians have to their land. When the land yields such flavorful products, it makes sense to use those products in the dishes that represent the island both at home and abroad.

FOODS OF THE INTERIOR

Since ancient times, Sardinia has been inhabited by shepherds and hunters. So, the cuisine of the interior has long been based on what the locals hunted, as well as shepherd traditions. Cheeses, roasted meats, wild herbs and vegetables, and long-lasting paper-thin bread prevail here. Dishes vary from village to village, but there are common elements such as the use of myrtle to flavor roasts, soups, and pastas and the use of fresh, seasonal vegetables such as wild asparagus in the early spring.

To outsiders, some Sardinian dishes may seem peculiar, but they make perfect sense when you consider that they have always been closely tied to the daily lives of Sardinians. Shepherds spent the summer months in the mountains, where they didn't have kitchens or cooking utensils, so they had to get creative. Unless they wanted to live on bread and cheese for months, they needed to find ways to prepare food out in the open. This gave rise to the custom of spit-roasting meat. The spits, which the shepherds made from the branches of trees and bushes, made the meat more flavorful. A roast of any kind, including suckling pig, wild boar, lamb, or goat, became the preferred meal of Sardinian shepherds and peasants and today remains a centerpiece of holiday meals.

The most appreciated animal of Sardinia, and the most commonly consumed meat, is lamb. Everywhere you go in Sardinia, the hills are dotted with sheep grazing peacefully on the flavorful Mediterranean herbs that give their milk and meat a particular flavor. Lamb is especially popular around Christmas and Easter—holidays for which Sardinians prepare a variety of rich, mostly meat-based dishes.

Sardinian sheep are a special breed recognized by the European Union with an IGP (*Indicazione Geografica Protetta* or Protected Geographical Indication) designation. The sheep whose milk is used for the production of pecorino are purebred; those raised for their meat are crossbred with other breeds.

Because Sardinia is usually associated with sheep, it might be easy to forget that raising cows and producing cheese from cow's milk is also a significant industry on the island, especially in the northwest and in

the area of Montiferru. Long ago, cattle were used primarily for field work, so the traditional Sardinian breed of cow was crossbred with a physically stronger cow from Modica in Sicily. The result is known as the Sardo-Modican breed, referred to locally as the *bue rosso*, or red bull. Its name comes from the beautiful brownish-red color of the cow's hide.

Once agriculture became mechanized, the *bue rosso* faced extinction, but thanks to the efforts of local farmers and the Slow Food community, these colorful animals continue to peacefully graze in the hills of Montiferru. Their delectable meat and *casizolu*, the flavorful cheese made from the milk of these unique cows, are recognized as *presidia* of the Slow Food movement.

The *bue rosso* survived because it is the only breed of cow raised in a completely natural way on the island, as the animals must be pastured. Every traveler to Sardinia should taste *casizolu*. Because the *bue rosso* has to be milked by hand, the cheese is more difficult to produce and less widely available than other cheeses. But if you're willing to venture into the hills of Montiferru, you can enjoy this Sardinian delicacy, which is still made by hand by local farmers.

Another well-known Sardinian delicacy is *porcheddu*, or spit-roasted suckling pig. Even meat lovers who have never visited the island dream of this succulent specialty—crunchy skin in perfect contrast with tender and delicate meat. The layer of fat under the skin melts during cooking, making the meat tender and delicious.

The suckling pig feeds mostly on its mother's milk, so its meat is tender, with a delicate flavor. Often, the meat is flavored with myrtle; the combination is unforgettable and utterly Sardinian. Each Sardinian cook has a different method for making *porcheddu* and jealously guards his secret (I say "his" because making *porcheddu* is decidedly the province of men). When in Sardinia, give in and let yourself be seduced by the incredible deliciousness of *porcheddu*.

Another animal common to the Sardinian landscape are goats, which often perch on rocky hillsides in gravity-defying poses. Goat meat is a common ingredient in Sardinian dishes, including pasta sauces, flavorful stews, or simple roasts. It has a slightly gamey flavor and a lean texture. Young goats that have fed only on their mothers' milk give particularly tender and flavorful meat.

Hunting has also contributed unique foods to the cuisine of the island. Wild boar, for instance, is a Christmas delicacy. Every Sardinian knows someone who hunts, and they often go to great lengths to procure a healthy piece of wild boar for a celebratory meal. The boar might be simply roasted, braised in wine, or turned into a delectable pasta sauce.

Sardinia also has a strong tradition of cured meats: prosciutto, salumi, and sausages are often enjoyed on their own with some bread and a glass of strong red wine, or used in pasta sauces and rustic soups. Sardinian sausages are simple and do not include common Italian sausage flavorings such as fennel; instead, coarsely ground or chopped meat is seasoned with salt, pepper, and occasionally crushed red pepper.

However, knowing about their simplicity leaves you unprepared for the sausages' extraordinary flavor. Butchers pride themselves on the flavor of their handmade sausages, and one bite explains why. The robust, yet natural, flavor and coarse texture give the sausages unmatched character. A common lunch for shepherds—as well as Sardinians of other occupations—is sausage, pecorino, bread, and a glass of red wine. Simple and delicious.

THE SEA AND ITS BOUNTY

The cuisine of the Sardinian coast is much younger than that of the interior. In the thirteenth century, the Genoese introduced the riches of the sea that up to then had remained unknown to the local population. To this day, the influence of the Genoese is visible in the many fish soups along the coast.

The coastal cuisine is also more open to outside influences, helping tell the story of the island and the many invasions. Over time, Sardinian cooks absorbed the influences of their invaders and incorporated them into their own cooking. Spicy Catalan lobster and paella are typical of Alghero, a seaside town on the west coast that retains some of the strongest Spanish influences. The Spaniards also brought the *cassola* of Cagliari, a fish soup, and *mazzamurru*, a bread-based soup eaten by Spanish sailors when the bread was old and needed to be softened.

The coastal cuisine is rich and varied: each part of Sardinia's 1,800-km coast seduces with noteworthy delicacies, roasted, grilled, or simply boiled. What you taste in Gallura, on the northern coast, will not be the same as the flavors of Cagliari or Oristano. Like the interior, the coast tells a story through its flavors, a story of inventiveness, varied traditions, and adaptation. From the mullet roe (*bottarga*) of Cabras to the tuna specialties of the island of San Pietro, seafood gives a new dimension to Sardinian cuisine, delighting those who come to the island expecting a true Mediterranean paradise.

FOOD AS TRADITION

Whether land-based or coastal, traditional Sardinian cooking is deeply rooted in culture, history, and traditions. For example, *porcheddu*, a hallmark of Sardinian cuisine, was originally cooked underground because the suckling pig was often acquired in suspect ways and had to be cooked without being noticed.

Another example of how life shaped Sardinian cuisine is *lobster alla catalana*, a specialty of Alghero: Lobster, an expensive ingredient, is cooked in an unusual style, with onion and tomatoes that cover its delicate flavor. This might seem strange today, but during their long fishing trips, the fishermen ate the lobsters that died aboard ship and aromatics such as onion improved the flavor. Likewise, crunchy, paper-thin *pane carasau* (Sardinian music sheet bread) was created because it was the only bread that didn't spoil during the months the shepherds spent in pasture. Soaked in broth or toasted over an open fire with some cheese, it sustained shepherds during their long absences from home.

Today, most restaurant menus showcase the richest dishes of Sardinia, and during holidays and festivities Sardinian cooks prepare magnificent feasts that feature these rich foods, including meats and a variety of tempting sweets. But for centuries the everyday cooking of Sardinia was anything but rich: Sardinian cooks used all their creativity to come up with interesting combinations of simple ingredients that could chase away their families' hunger pangs. The dishes that developed through the ages on this poor and isolated island were simple and made great use of local ingredients. Many of the dishes were based on

legumes, an affordable source of protein. Fish, meat, and sweets were used much less often.

Poverty also ensured that nothing went to waste. To this day, Sardinian cooks proudly make use of each part of the animal. In fact, internal organs are a prized holiday delicacy, and blood sausage is a traditional dish.

Poverty had other effects on Sardinia's cuisine as well. Sardinians have a ritualistic attitude toward food, insisting on sharing it with others at all costs. In the past, this generosity saved many from hunger. Today, when hunger isn't the issue it has been in the past, sharing food with others remains a sign of friendship and hospitality that can often surprise the uninitiated visitor.

When you are invited to a Sardinian's home for a meal, get ready for an unforgettable experience. The most delicious Sardinian foods are found in the kitchens of mothers and grandmothers. The memories of tasting those dishes in the company of Sardinian families are the best souvenirs any traveler could hope for.

BREAD

The place of honor on every Sardinian table is reserved not for delicacies, such as lobster or *bottarga*, but for one of the simplest foods: bread. Bread has sustained generations of Sardinians and remains an important part of their diet. In the past, when Sardinia was poor, much of the population survived on one meal a day, which was usually consumed in the evening. The meal often consisted of little more than vegetable soup; to make it through the rest of the day, Sardinians relied on a lunchtime snack of bread, cheese, and an occasional artichoke.

When there was nothing else available, bread would quiet the hunger pangs. So, it's not surprising that bread has acquired deep, symbolic meaning and inspires reverence among Sardinians. If a piece of bread, no matter how small, falls to the ground, an older Sardinian will likely pick it up and kiss it. In Sardinia, bread is a gift.

Bread became so important to Sardinians that brides had to demonstrate their bread-making skills before marriage. Over the centuries, hundreds of types of bread developed: some were reserved for special

occasions (mostly religious), others for celebrations, still others for everyday use. The different breads vary not as much in the dough as in the decorations that developed to celebrate the different occasions. Each town and village has its own traditional shapes that have been passed down for generations and cannot be found anywhere else. Forced to survive on bread, Sardinians poured their imagination into it and created thousands of complicated shapes. Some of the traditional Sardinian breads are so beautiful that one is reluctant to break off a piece.

The most famous bread in Sardinia is *pane carasau*, also known as *carta da musica* (music sheet): paper-thin crisp rounds of dough that can last for months. Today, *pane carasau* is made all over the island, often in large factories. Originally, the bread was made exclusively in Ogliastra, in the interior of the island, and making it by hand required at least two days of hard work. *Pane carasau* is made from semolina (durum wheat) flour and water. In the past, it was made with no yeast; instead, it was left to leaven for a long time. The extended leavening period developed a richer, more complex flavor.

After being rolled out into paper-thin sheets, the bread is baked in a hot wood-burning oven, where it puffs up and separates into two layers. After the two layers are cut and separated from each other, they are returned to the oven to become toasted and crispy. Because it is baked twice, *pane carasau* loses all of its moisture and can be stored for months without going moldy.

Today, *pane carasau* has many uses in Sardinian cuisine. It can be served with various toppings and even made into desserts. It is also used to thicken soups; many Sardinians enjoy it even for breakfast, dipped in milk and coffee. When toasted and drizzled with olive oil, *pane carasau* is known as *pane guttiau*, which makes a perfect snack: crunchy bread with the earthy flavor of Sardinian olive oil. *Pane frattau* is *pane carasau* soaked in broth and served with tomato sauce and pecorino. But this description doesn't even begin to do justice to the complexity of the flavors of this dish: eating *pane frattau* in Sardinia is not simply nourishment, it is tasting tradition.

Thicker and slightly harder than *pane carasau* is *pane pistoccu*, which was traditionally consumed by shepherds in the Sarrabus and Ogliastra regions.

Pane civraxiu is circular in shape and has a dark, thick crust and a soft center. It's perfect for wiping a plate clean. *Pane spianada* (or *spianata*) of Gallura is a circular loaf, similar to a Middle Eastern pita, that used to be decorated and served at feasts but is now eaten on an everyday basis.

The list goes on. Each village and town produces unique shapes of bread, such as animals, dolls, doves for weddings, and crosses for Easter.

Today, most Sardinian breads are commercially produced, but many Sardinian cooks still make bread at home, and small bakeries still rely on the artisanal process and natural leavening traditions of the past. Tasting Sardinian bread is an experience worth a trip to the island. You'll love the rich flavor of durum wheat and sense the tradition poured into every loaf. It's like tasting history.

Other bread-like foods with unique flavors are common to Sardinia. *Fainé*, which is related to Ligurian *farinata* (a thick chickpea flour pancake made in large, round pans and baked in a pizza oven), is most commonly found in Sassari, but you'll find it in Alghero too. Plain (containing only chickpea flour, water, oil, and salt) or with onions, sausage, or mushrooms, it is the perfect snack and worth seeking out.

CHEESE

Vast pasture lands blanketed in fragrant Mediterranean brush, intense sun and favorable winds, and traditional methods of production all make Sardinian cheeses memorable and unique. Sardinia is most famous for its sheep's milk cheeses—commonly known as pecorino—but the cheeses made from cow's and goat's milk are no less delicious.

When you have the good fortune to taste a piece of aged pecorino and the herbal flavors explode in your mouth, you'll understand why Sardinian pecorino is one of the most widely appreciated products both on the island and around the world. Sardinia produces about 70 percent of all Italian-made pecorino. Needless to say, cheese is an important economic resource for the island.

The three most well-known and widely appreciated Sardinian cheeses are made from sheep's milk: *pecorino sardo, pecorino romano,* and *fiore sardo*. All three are DOP (*Denominazione di Origine Protetta*) products, which means that they are recognized by the government of Italy and the European Union as unique products closely tied to the traditions of the place where they are produced.

The several million sheep that graze in the pastures of Sardinia are part of the charm of its landscape. Everywhere you go, you'll hear their

bells even before you see them dotting the bright green hillsides. Even today sheep in Sardinia are tended in the traditional way; they spend the summer in the mountains, enjoying somewhat cooler weather and delicious Mediterranean herbs. In the fall, they come down the mountain sides into the plains, repeating a centuries-old ritual that has disappeared from most other places. Sardinian shepherds are the keepers of some of the most remarkable traditions of the island. These hardworking, solitary people intimately familiar with nature and its rhythms continue to follow traditions that make it possible for them to produce flavorful cheeses with unique character.

Pecorino sardo DOP, which is made from the milk of Sardinian sheep in the traditional way, comes in two varieties: *dolce* (young, which is meant to be eaten about a month after being made) or *maturo* (mature, or aged for 2 to 12 months). *Pecorino sardo dolce* is mild, creamy, and melts easily, so it is perfect for pasta with cheese (the Sardinian equivalent of mac 'n' cheese). *Pecorino sardo maturo* is a harder cheese that is usually grated to finish a pasta dish, but is also delicious as a snack. It is stronger in flavor and grainier in texture, which makes it perfect to enjoy with a glass of red wine or one of the unique Sardinian wines enjoyed at the end of a meal, such as Malvasia di Bosa.

Most *pecorino romano*—a cheese whose name unequivocally recalls Rome—is also produced in Sardinia. *Pecorino romano* has been exported by the island for centuries. Because of the close traditional ties between Genoa and Sardinia, pesto, the Genoese condiment *par excellence*, is often made with *pecorino romano*.

The most distinctive Sardinian pecorino is *fiore sardo*, which is made the same way today as it has been for centuries, from raw whole sheep's milk with lamb rennet. It is aged for several months in a damp place and often smoked over herbs. When young, *fiore sardo* is often served as an *antipasto*. When it is aged, the hints of Mediterranean herbs and dried fruit become more pronounced. It is an excellent dessert cheese, but it also adds complexity to pasta dishes if grated on right before serving.

Another notable Sardinian pecorino is *pecorino gran cru.* This extraordinary cheese is the result of a collaboration between Academia Barilla, which promotes authentic Italian food products made by reputable artisans, and Latteria Sociale Cooperativa San Pasquale in Nulvi, a cooperative of small sheep farms. This strong-flavored pecorino is made from the milk of sheep that graze on the very best pastures of wild herbs in the hills of northwestern Sardinia. Bold flavors of Mediterranean herbs and grasses come through in the cheese, which is both savory and sweet. Its flavors are intensified by an aging period of more than 20 months. As the cheese matures, its flavors deepen and the texture becomes slightly grainy, reminding one of a great parmigiano-reggiano with the added richness that comes from sheep's milk. *Pecorino gran cru* is best enjoyed on its own, as a snack or *antipasto*, or to end a great meal. It pairs beautifully with a glass of dessert wine.

While pecorino is made throughout the island, other cheeses have more specific provenance. *Casizolu*, a cow's milk cheese, is still produced in a labor-intensive, traditional way in the area of Montiferru. The familiar pear shape of the cheese is a welcome sight on every table. The cheese is mild and almost sweet, so it is often served for breakfast with fresh bread and Sardinian honey. The *casizolu* produced from the milk of the *bue rosso*, or red bull, (a breed of cow unique to Sardinia with a brown-red hide) is a rare treat worthy of a trip to Sardinia.

The list of Sardinian cheeses goes on. Ricotta, which can be made from cow's, sheep's, or goat's milk, comes in several varieties: *gentile* (sweet and not aged), *salata* (salted and pressed, usually used for grating), and *mustia* (dry and smoked). Less well known are the flavorful, delicious goat's milk cheeses (*caprini*).

Some of these cheeses are so deeply rooted in tradition that they are only available in specific areas or at specific times of the year. But cheese lovers, Sardinian and foreign, know how truly special these cheeses are and seek them out, patiently waiting for the right time.

One Sardinian cheese that takes particular dedication and persistence to find is the legendary *casu marzu* (pecorino with maggots)—most certainly an acquired taste. Traditionally, shepherds made the cheese by saving pecorino that had become infested with maggots and allowing it to rot. The maggots eat the inside of the cheese and digest it, which turns it into a creamy substance with a pungent flavor. Today, this cheese is illegal to sell, but you can find it through friends with shepherd connections.

Even if you decide to pass on the *casu marzu*, there are plenty of other cheeses to enjoy in this cheese-lover's paradise.

Sardinian Ingredients

BOTTARGA

Sardinian food, while closely tied to the history of poverty on the island, is not characterized exclusively by simple and affordable ingredients. Take, for instance, *bottarga*, which is a salted and dried fish roe aptly known as "Sardinian caviar." *Bottarga* is a delicacy in coastal areas. On the island of San Pietro in the southwest, which is famous for tuna fishing and the yearly *mattanza* (tuna hunt), fishermen make *bottarga* from tuna roe. Oristano and Cabras, on the west coast of Sardinia, are famous for gray mullet *bottarga* (*bottarga di muggine*).

Cabras is famous for its ponds, which have served for centuries as the spawning ground for mullet. Mullet *bottarga* is strong in flavor, with the salty aroma characteristic of the sea. It is still made in the traditional way by using sea salt and drying the roe in special furnaces at very low temperatures. This concentrates the flavors and intensifies the salinity. The labor-intensive process of producing *bottarga* makes it a pricey ingredient. But a little *bottarga* goes a long way: its strong and concentrated flavor adds complexity to dishes and makes them more robust, so a grating of *bottarga* on pasta is all you need.

Bottarga can elevate the simplest salad or pasta dish to new heights, lending depth of flavor and salinity. For this reason, it is often compared to the truffles of northern Italy. Grated on spaghetti tossed with a little extra virgin olive oil, *bottarga* became one of the most famous dishes of the island. Sliced thinly, it can also be served as an appetizer. It pairs well with full-bodied wines with that distinct savory character, such as *Vernaccia di Oristano* or *Malvasia di Bosa*.

EXTRA VIRGIN OLIVE OIL

Bread and olive oil, staples in all Italian regions, may not be uniquely Sardinian, but in Sardinia, these simple ingredients reach new heights. The island's countless types of bread and flavorful extra virgin olive oils elevate each meal to a memorable experience. When a basket of toasted *pane carasau* drizzled with flavorful olive oil arrives on the table, no one can resist.

Sardinian olive oil is robust in flavor with notes of artichoke, a common vegetable on the island. The most famous Sardinian olive oil comes from the slopes of Montiferru, where oil is still made in the traditional way and the olive trees are not commonly sprayed with chemicals. Montiferru extra virgin olive oil is a perfect condiment for Sardinian dishes—it accentuates the flavor of green vegetables and adds complexity to pasta and meats.

HONEY

Sardinian honey is another unrivaled delicacy. I have never seen as many different types of honey as I encountered in Sardinia: from artichoke and cardoon to myrtle, citrus, and *corbezzolo* (often translated as "strawberry-tree"), there is a honey for every occasion. The varieties are boundless, and each honey has a distinct flavor and personality, ranging from sweet and flowery to dark, bitter, and robust. The island is a paradise for bees and beekeepers. In spring, when flowers and trees are in bloom, bees are everywhere, working hard to make delicious honey.

When in Sardinia, I enjoy honey at least a couple of times a day. In the morning, with fresh bread and *casizolu* (a mild cow's milk cheese), I love *miele di asfodelo*, which is delicate, flowery, and sweet. *Miele di corbezzolo* is the rarest and most typical honey of Sardinia. The *corbezzolo* is a Mediterranean tree that flowers in the winter, from November to February. The cold weather makes the bees' work significantly more difficult. Thus, *miele di corbezzolo* is difficult to produce and therefore difficult to find. But, when you do find it, make a point to taste it. It is a unique experience. After a meal, I drizzle *miele di corbezzolo* on

sebadas. The bitterness of the honey contrasts nicely with the robust, cheese-filled pastry.

SAFFRON

The pride and joy of Sardinia is its saffron, which recently received a DOP designation. The best saffron comes from San Gavino Monreale, in the southern region of Campidano. This unique, aromatic spice, probably brought to the island by the Spaniards, has found its way into fresh pasta, sauces, soups, and even roasts and desserts. The orange color and unmistakable aroma of saffron permeate Sardinian food and imprint themselves in the memory of the visitor—one more badge of honor for this interesting island.

SUNDRIED TOMATOES

Sardinian cooks often use sundried tomatoes, packed in salt, to add flavor to sauces and soups. Sardinian tomatoes are sweet and flavorful, but because the tomato season is relatively short, Sardinians dry these delicacies and preserve them in salt. Dried slowly in the hot Mediterranean sun, the tomatoes' flavors become concentrated. They taste like pure sunshine when added to any dish.

You can make your own sundried tomatoes. Select very ripe, flavorful tomatoes, wash them well, and cut them into halves lengthwise. Place them on a tray, cut side up. Sprinkle abundantly with sea salt and let them dry in the sun for 3 to 4 days. When the tomatoes are completely dry, store them in a jar in a cool, dry place for up to several months.

Wine

When it comes to wine, Sardinia is like a continent. Although it is relatively small, the island grows an incredible variety of grapes and produces diverse styles of wine: from crisp and refreshing whites to full-bodied reds to concentrated sweet wines best enjoyed at the end of the meal with aged pecorino.

Sardinia has a centuries-long tradition of winemaking. It is a sunny place where grapes ripen easily. Yet Sardinian wines are not well known outside the island. Traditionally, many Sardinian wines—especially those made from the rare native grapes—were consumed only locally. More recently, some of the larger wineries have found an export market for these intriguing, unusual wines.

Many of the grapes that grow on the island likely originated in Spain and were brought to Sardinia during the 400-year Spanish rule. In Sardinia's poor soils, these grapes find their true expression and produce wines that are unique and full of character—wines that can capture the imagination of even the most discriminating wine drinkers.

The most famous Sardinian grapes are white vermentino and red cannonau (known as grenache outside of Italy). Vermentino grows all over the island, but it has found its spiritual home in the northeastern region of Gallura. Vermentino grown anywhere on the island can be labeled Vermentino di Sardegna DOC. If the grapes are grown in Gallura only, the wine can be labeled Vermentino di Gallura DOCG (one of a handful of Italian whites at the highest level of the Italian wine classification system: *Denominazione di Origine Controllata e Garantita*).

Vermentino grapes traditionally produced full-bodied wines that were high in alcohol. In recent times, producers have learned to tame the alcohol and now make crisp whites from vermentino that are refreshing and unique in flavor. Typically, *Vermentino* has aromas and flavors of Mediterranean brush and citrus, with a slight aftertaste of bitter almond—all flavors that remind the drinker of the wine's Mediterranean heritage. It pairs well with light vegetable appetizers and many fish dishes. To showcase the potential of the vermentino grape

CAPICHERA
VT
Giovannella & Alberto Ragnedda
Arzachena, Italia

CAPICHERA

NIEDDERA
CONTINI

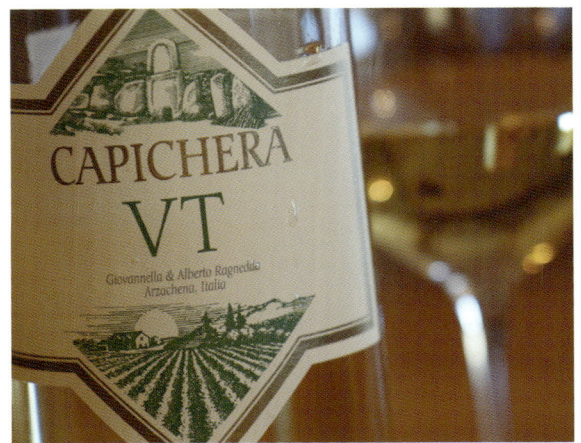

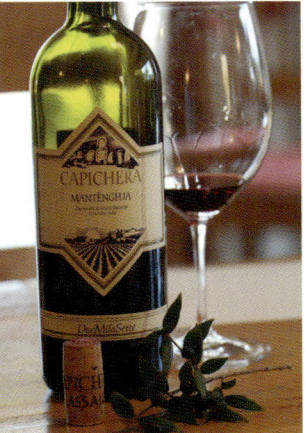

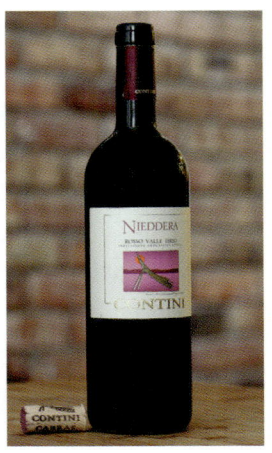

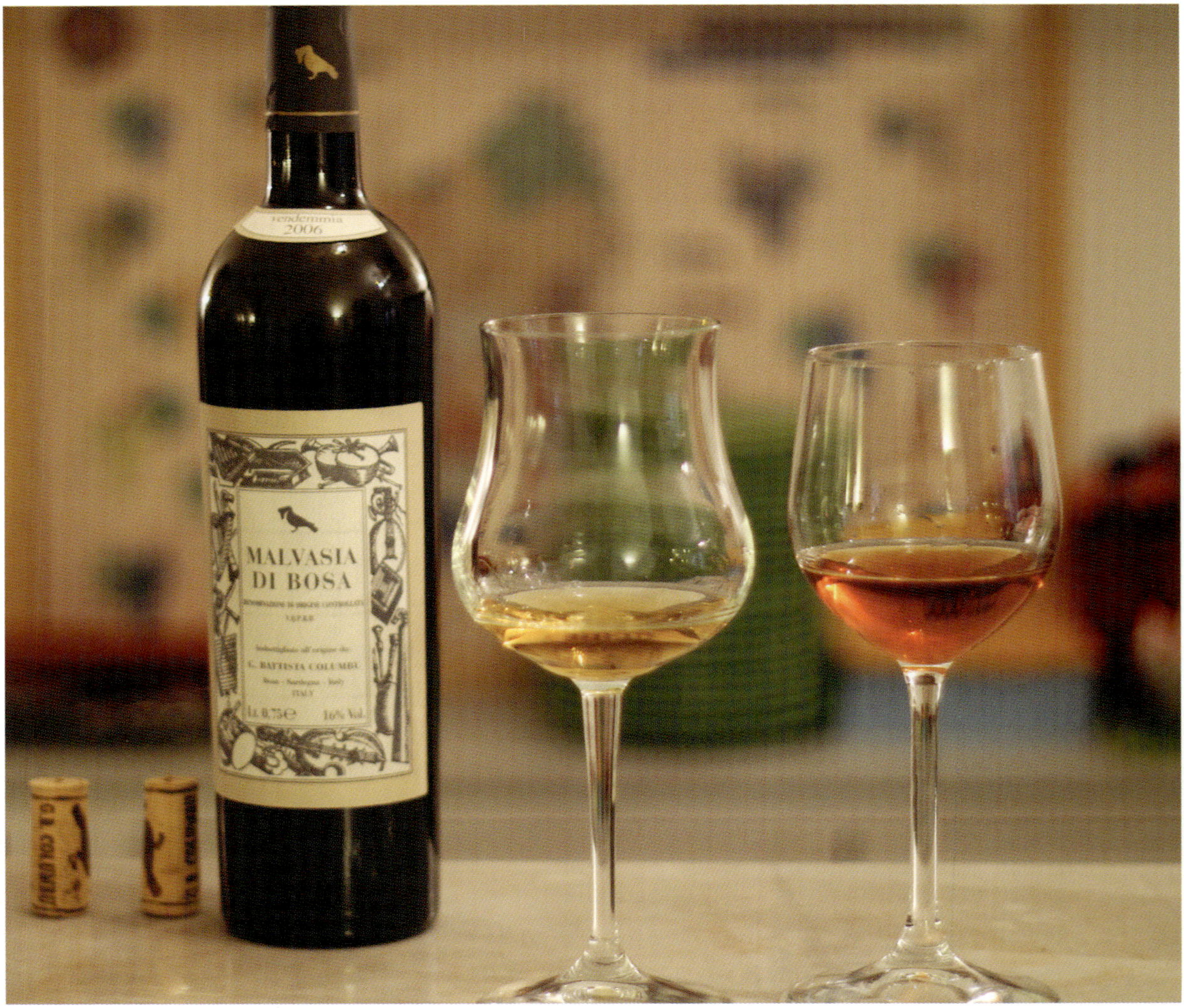
vendemmia
2006
MALVASIA
DI BOSA

and its relationship to the territory, some producers bottle higher-end and even single-vineyard *Vermentino* wines. Capichera, a high-quality producer of *Vermentino* in Gallura, makes a stunning single-vineyard *Vermentino* with a strong backbone of acidity and minerality. A wine full of personality, it is one of the few whites that age beautifully.

Other ancient white grape varieties thrive in certain areas of the island. In the north and northwest, you'll find torbato (tourbat in France), an aromatic white. Sella & Mosca, the island's largest wine producer, makes a dry version and also a sparkling brut from the grape.

In the south, the native white grape nuragus produces light, crisp wines that pair well with calamari and other lemony seafood, and also drink beautifully on their own on a hot summer day. Think of wines from nuragus as the Italian equivalent of Portugal's *Vinho Verde*.

Another white grape grown in the south is nasco. In the past, nasco was made into a sweet wine, but some wineries (most notably, Argiolas) showcase the potential of this native grape by producing crisp dry whites.

On to red wines. The most famous Sardinian red grape, cannonau, grows all over the island, but it is best suited to the mountains around Oliena and Jerzu. Here, it produces full-bodied reds that pair well with the more robust foods of the interior. This wine, which has traditionally been the red wine of choice among islanders, is now made in less rustic and lighter, more balanced versions that appeal more to the international market. The best versions combine the flavors of wild berries with more earthy tobacco and tar notes, along with a hint of Mediterranean herbs.

Another red grape that produces interesting wines is monica. Monica wines are berry-like, lighter, and more aromatic than those made from cannonau. The best monica wines are found north of Cagliari.

The area of Sulcis in the southwest is the spiritual home of carignano (in France, carignan). It produces full-bodied, well-structured reds that pair perfectly with meat roasts and aged cheeses. *Carignano* is one of the Sardinian reds that can age well and keeps developing in complexity. Sardus Pater and Santadi, both located in Sulcis, produce several good versions. Capichera, a winery best known for its *Vermentino*, also produces memorable reds from carignano.

Thriving in the north, around Sassari, cagnulari is yet another red grape that produces distinctive wines. The berry flavors blend with notes of forest floor and even smoke. The best wines from cagnulari are seductive, yet firm. Cecchi, a winery in Usini, produces memorable *Cagnulari*, but its wines cannot be found in North America. Alas, to taste this interesting red, you'll have to go to Sardinia.

A native grape that has gained much popularity recently is bovale sardo. Today, bovale sardo is rarely found on its own. Most often, it is blended with other red grapes, such as cannonau and monica. Korem, an excellent full-bodied red produced by Argiolas, is a blend based on bovale sardo.

In addition to white and red wines, Sardinia also produces wines similar in style to Spanish sherry. The province of Oristano boasts one of Sardinia's most ancient and interesting wines, Vernaccia di Oristano DOC. Like Spanish sherry, it is a dry wine aged under a layer of *flor*, which gives it savory aromas of almond and olive. Depending on its age, it can be amber or golden yellow and is usually high in alcohol (15% to 18%). It is an after-dinner drink to be savored on its own, even though lighter versions pair well with strongly flavored foods, such as *bottarga*. The historic winery Attilio Contini produces a range of *Vernaccia* wines worth seeking out, as well as other interesting whites and reds.

Another Sardinian wine that has reached cult status is *Malvasia di Bosa*, a complex wine with an astounding richness of flavor. *Malvasia* is among the most interesting Italian "meditation" wines, wines to be enjoyed slowly at the end of the meal. Production of *Malvasia di Bosa* is very limited, so not much of this wine leaves the island—but it is so unique that it alone merits a trip to Sardinia. A visit to the historic winery of Columbu, in the center of Bosa, is a unique experience that can make anyone a believer in *Malvasia di Bosa*.

From light and crisp *Vermentino* to full-bodied *Cannonau* to amber, nectar-like *Vernaccia* and *Malvasia*, Sardinia abounds in enticing wines for a range of tastes. As you enjoy the recipes in this book, seek out wines I recommend to accompany them. Then, you will taste the true essence of Sardinia—foods and wines that have developed together over centuries and dance on the palate in perfect harmony.

LIQUEURS

Sardinia is also famous for a variety of liqueurs, from sweet *mirto* to anise– and prickly pear–flavored *acquavite* to sweet *limoncello*. In the past, most liqueurs were made at home, with each maker adding flavors that appealed most to his or her palate. Today, more and more liqueurs are produced on a commercial scale and can be found outside the island, but the true gems are the artisanal products.

Mirto, Sardinia's national drink, is a sweet liqueur made from the fragrant purple berries of the myrtle bush. It is potent, but also smooth. It is the perfect ending to a Sardinian meal and pairs well with rich desserts. In Sardinia, *mirto* is also often enjoyed as an *aperitivo*, before the meal.

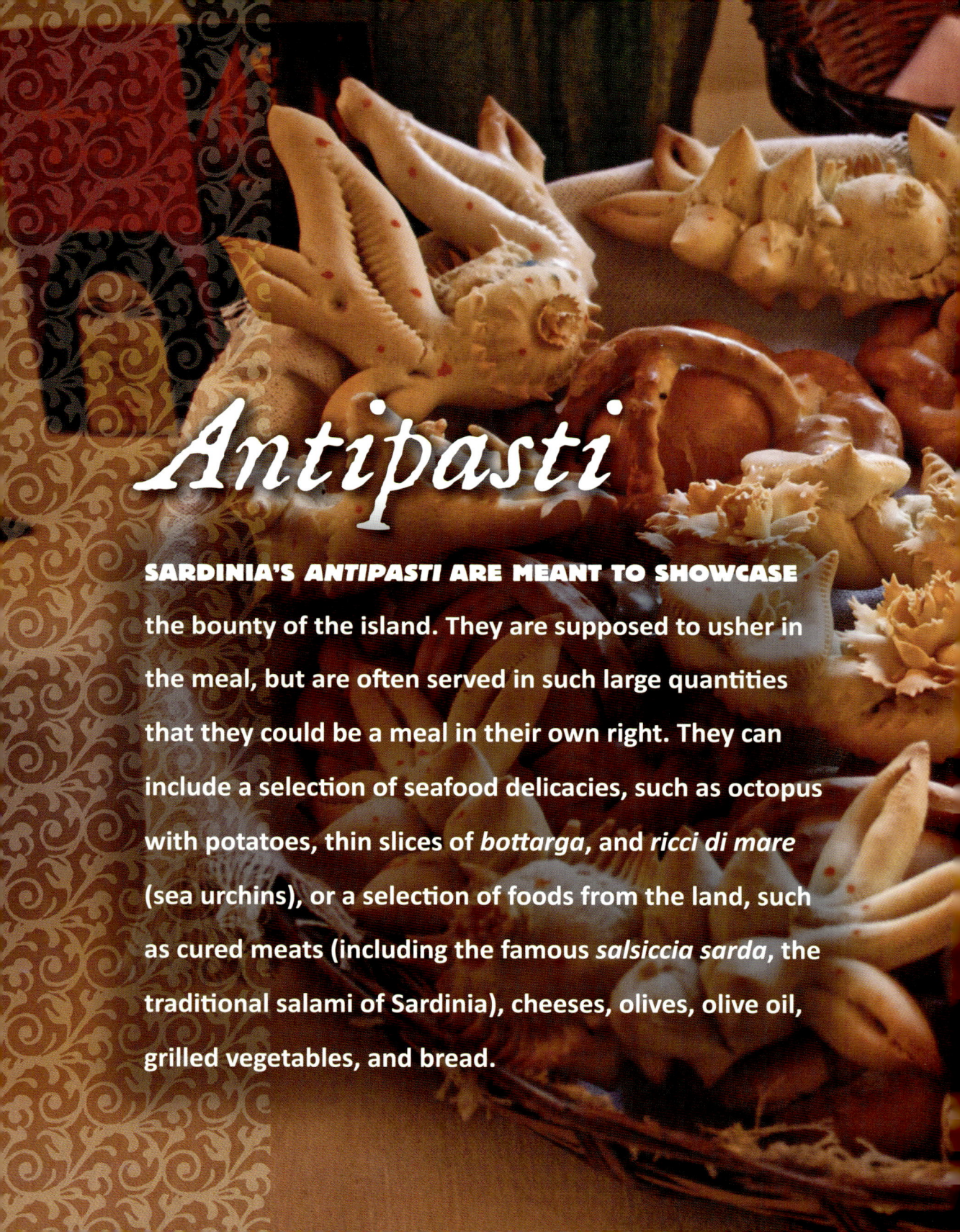

Antipasti

SARDINIA'S *ANTIPASTI* ARE MEANT TO SHOWCASE the bounty of the island. They are supposed to usher in the meal, but are often served in such large quantities that they could be a meal in their own right. They can include a selection of seafood delicacies, such as octopus with potatoes, thin slices of *bottarga*, and *ricci di mare* (sea urchins), or a selection of foods from the land, such as cured meats (including the famous *salsiccia sarda*, the traditional salami of Sardinia), cheeses, olives, olive oil, grilled vegetables, and bread.

Artichokes with *Bottarga*

Fresh artichokes are a much-appreciated delicacy in Sardinia. Their green heads greet you from market stalls and dot the horizon around Oristano, tempting the taste buds. They are often paired with another local delicacy, bottarga. *The strong, savory flavor of* bottarga, *dried and salted fish roe, enriches the crunchy, fresh artichokes, bringing together land and sea. I always use Sardinian olive oil in this dish, as it complements the flavor of the artichokes. In particular, oil from Montiferru, which boasts aromas and flavors of artichokes, is a great complement to the dish.*

The perfect wine pairing for this dish is Contini Karmis, a robust, almost savory white that is a blend of vernaccia and vermentino. The vermentino in the wine complements the flavor of the artichokes, a notoriously difficult food to pair with wine, and the richness of the vernaccia matches that of the bottarga.

YIELD: 4 SERVINGS

- 4 fresh raw artichokes, cleaned and thinly sliced
- Sea salt and freshly ground black pepper, to taste
- 2–3 teaspoons grated *bottarga*
- 2 tablespoons extra virgin olive oil

1. Layer the artichoke slices on a serving platter.
2. Sprinkle the artichokes lightly with the salt, black pepper, and *bottarga*.
3. Drizzle with the oil and serve immediately at room temperature.

Burrida, Cagliari-Style

Burrida *is a traditional Sardinian seafood* antipasto *that is always served cold. There are two main versions: In Oristano, on the west coast, it is made with tomato sauce, and in Cagliari, in the south, it is made with walnuts and white wine vinegar, but no tomatoes. The fish traditionally used in* burrida *is either dogfish (*gattuccio*), a firm-fleshed fish that belongs to the shark family, or skate. I use skate, but if skate is difficult to find, you can also use any other firm-fleshed fish, such as swordfish.*

This unique and flavorful dish pairs well with Dettori Romangia Bianco, a unique white wine made from vermentino grapes. The wine is not clarified or filtered, so it may contain some sediment; it benefits from being opened a couple of hours before serving. Dettori Romangia Bianco has a strong personality, which matches the character of the dish. It's a true Sardinian experience!

YIELD: 4–6 SERVINGS

- 1 pound (454 g) skate, cut into 1-inch (2.5-cm) pieces
- 2 quarts (1.90 L) water
- 1 teaspoon sea salt, plus more, to taste
- ½ cup (119 mL) plus 2 tablespoons white wine vinegar, divided
- 3 tablespoons (45 mL) extra virgin olive oil
- 2 cloves garlic, minced
- 2 tablespoons finely chopped fresh parsley
- 20 kernels walnuts, chopped
- ¼ cup (59 mL) dry white wine
- Freshly ground black pepper, to taste

1. Wash the skate in cold water and pat it dry with a paper towel. Set aside.
2. In a medium (8- to 12-quart [7.6- to 11.4-L]) stockpot, bring the water, 1 teaspoon of salt, and 2 tablespoons of the vinegar to a boil.
3. Add the skate, reduce the heat to low, and boil gently for 4 to 6 minutes, until the fish is cooked through. Drain and set aside to cool.
4. In a small (2- to 3-quart [1.9- to 2.8-L]) sauté pan, warm the oil and garlic over medium-low heat. When the garlic starts to sizzle, add the parsley and cook for 2 minutes.
5. Add the remaining ½ cup (119 mL) white wine vinegar and cook over medium heat for 2 minutes, until the vinegar starts to evaporate.
6. Add the walnuts and a pinch of salt, stirring well. Add the wine and raise the heat to high. Cook for 3 to 4 minutes, until the alcohol in the wine evaporates.
7. Reduce the heat to low and continue to cook for 7 to 8 minutes, until the sauce thickens. Remove from the heat. Add the black pepper. Adjust the seasoning to taste.
8. In a shallow dish or bowl, combine the fish and the sauce, cover tightly with plastic wrap, and refrigerate for at least 8 hours (and up to 2 days) before serving. Serve chilled.

Burrida, Oristano-Style

This dish pairs well with a light Vermentino with good acidity, such as Contini Tyrsos: a light, yet flavorful wine that beautifully ushers in the meal.

YIELD: 4–6 SERVINGS

- 1 pound (454 g) skate, cut into 1-inch (2.5-cm) pieces
- 2 quarts (1.90 L) water
- 1 teaspoon sea salt, plus more, to taste
- 1 cup (237 mL) white wine vinegar
- 1 tablespoon extra virgin olive oil
- 1 clove garlic, thinly sliced
- 1 (14-ounce [397-g]) can tomatoes, chopped

1. Wash the skate in cold water and pat it dry with a paper towel. Set aside.
2. In a medium (8- to 12-quart [7.6- to 11.4-L]) stockpot, bring the water, 1 teaspoon of salt, and the vinegar to a boil.
3. Add the skate, reduce the heat to medium, and cook for 4 to 6 minutes, until the skate is cooked through. Drain and set aside to cool.
4. In a medium (4- to 5-quart [3.8- to 4.7-L]) sauté pan, warm the oil and garlic until the garlic starts to sizzle.
5. Add the tomatoes, stir well, and bring to a boil.
6. Reduce the heat to low and cook for 15 to 20 minutes, until the sauce reduces by about ¼. Remove from the heat. Season with salt to taste. Cool.
7. In a shallow dish or bowl, combine the skate and the cool tomato sauce. Cover tightly with plastic wrap.
8. Refrigerate for at least 2 hours (and up to 2 days) before serving. Serve chilled.

Deviled Eggs

In typical Sardinian fashion, these deviled eggs are simple and delicious. The vinegar adds acidity, making the dish lighter, and the breadcrumbs add texture, making it more complex. Pair with a full-bodied white wine, such as Contini Karmis, for the perfect balance of richness and flavor.

YIELD: 6–12 SERVINGS

- **6 hardboiled eggs, peeled and cut into halves**
- **1 tablespoon vinegar (red or white wine)**
- **1 tablespoon extra virgin olive oil**
- **1 whole clove garlic**
- **2 tablespoons Homemade Breadcrumbs (see recipe on p. 65)**
- **½ tablespoon minced fresh parsley**
- **Sea salt, to taste**

1. Place the egg halves on a serving platter. Sprinkle each egg half with a little vinegar.
2. In a medium (4- to 5-quart [3.8- to 4.7-L]) sauté pan, warm the oil and garlic. When the garlic starts to sizzle, take it out and discard it.
3. Add the breadcrumbs and stir well. Toast the breadcrumbs over medium-low heat until they are light brown, stirring constantly to prevent burning.
4. Remove the sauté pan from the heat. Add the parsley and season with salt to taste.
5. Divide the breadcrumb mixture evenly over the egg halves. Serve warm or at room temperature.

Focaccia Sarda

This focaccia is easy to make and extra delicious. The pecorino gives it a more robust flavor and the tomatoes balance that richness. It is perfect as a snack or instead of bread. It also makes perfect picnic fare and pairs well with cheese, olives, and cured meats. Baking the focaccia on a pizza stone makes the bottom crispier and crunchier, just like you'd experience in Sardinia.

YIELD: 4–8 SERVINGS

- ½ pound (227 g) russet potatoes, peeled and cubed (about 1½ cups)
- 2 teaspoons sea salt, divided
- 1 cup (237 mL) warm milk
- 1½ cups (188 g) all-purpose flour
- 1 (¼-ounce [7-g]) packet quick-rise dry yeast
- 2 tablespoons plus ¼ cup (59 mL) extra virgin olive oil, divided
- 1 small onion, chopped (about ¾ cup [113 g])
- 1½ cups (240 g) quartered ripe cherry or grape tomatoes
- ½ cup (50 g) freshly grated pecorino, for sprinkling

1. In a medium (8- to 12-quart [7.6- to 11.4-L]) stockpot, cover the potatoes with water to about ½ inch (13 mm) above the potatoes. Add 1½ teaspoons of the salt and bring to a boil. Cook until a fork goes through the potatoes easily. Remove from the heat. Drain and mash the potatoes.
2. In a small bowl, combine the mashed potatoes with the milk. Stir well. Set aside.
3. In a medium bowl, combine the flour and yeast. Add the potato mixture to the flour mixture, stirring well with a wooden spoon until the ingredients are combined and the dough is uniform. The dough should be soft.
4. Cover the bowl with a kitchen towel, wrap it in a blanket, and let it rise in a warm place for at least 2 hours. The dough should roughly double in size.
5. Preheat the oven to 375°F (190°C).
6. In a medium (4- to 5-quart [3.8- to 4.7-L]) sauté pan, warm 2 tablespoons of the oil over medium heat. Add the onion and cook for 3 to 4 minutes, until it starts to soften.
7. Add the tomatoes and the remaining ½ teaspoon salt and cook for 4 minutes, until the tomatoes have released their liquid. Set aside.

8. Line a 9 × 11-inch (22.5 × 27.5-cm) baking dish with aluminum foil. Brush the foil abundantly with ¼ cup (59 mL) olive oil. Distribute the dough evenly in the prepared dish.
9. Spread the tomato mixture on top. Sprinkle with the pecorino.
10. Bake for 1 hour, until both the bottom and top of the focaccia are golden and crisp. Remove from the oven.
11. Transfer to a serving platter and serve hot.

FAVA

Fava (also known as broad beans) are one of the first vegetables to become available each spring, and Europeans have been rejoicing over their arrival in the markets since ancient times. Fava are one of the first plants ever cultivated, and they were the only beans the Europeans knew before the many varieties grown in the Americas were discovered.

Naturally high in fiber and iron, they are often referred to as the "meat of the poor" because they are so high in protein. To this day, Sardinians impatiently await the arrival of the first fava and enjoy them in a variety of ways, including raw with a shaving of pecorino and cooked.

Fresh Fava with Mint

On a hot, sunny day in May, we stopped at a roadside vegetable stand to pick up some fresh fava. The vendor, who was tired of sitting under the unrelenting sun, tried to convince me to buy all he had—5 kilos (about 11 pounds) or so. To make his case, he explained how they eat fava in and around Nuragus—simply boiled with salt and mint.

"Olive oil?" I asked.

"Nooo," he vehemently shook his head. "No olive oil whatsoever."

Having never tried plain boiled fava without oil, I doubted him. Maybe he had missed something?

When I asked my friends in Nuragus, they confirmed what the vendor had told me: No oil is used to prepare fava in Nuragus. One bite of the dish convinced me that there's no need. When the ingredients are so tasty, they stand on their own, as every Sardinian knows. Serve this dish with a medium-bodied white wine, such as Cantina di Mogoro Ajò, which is made from the nuragus grape that grows around Cagliari.

YIELD: 4 SERVINGS

- 2 quarts (1.90 L) water
- 1 pound (454 g) fresh fava, shelled, but with outer membrane
- Sea salt, to taste
- 2 tablespoons chopped fresh mint

1. In a medium (8- to 12-quart [7.6- to 11.4-L]) stockpot, bring the water to a boil. Add the fava and boil for 2 to 3 minutes, until they start to soften. Remove from the heat.
2. Drain the fava and set them aside to cool. Remove the outer membrane of each bean (if necessary).
3. Sprinkle with the salt and mint and serve at room temperature or chilled.

Herbed Breadcrumbs

Fried breadcrumbs are the perfect flavor enhancer for soups, pasta, and salads. They also add a slight crunch, making the texture of a dish more interesting. The herbs in these pan-fried breadcrumbs provide concentrated aromas, elevating the dish to new heights. These breadcrumbs can be made several days ahead and kept in an airtight container in the fridge.

YIELD: 1/2 CUP (60 G) BREADCRUMBS

- 2 tablespoons extra virgin olive oil
- 1 clove garlic, finely minced
- 1 teaspoon finely minced fresh mint
- 1 tablespoon finely minced fresh parsley
- 1 tablespoon finely minced fresh arugula
- Sea salt and freshly ground black pepper, to taste
- ½ cup (54 g) Homemade Breadcrumbs (recipe follows)

1. In a small (2- to 3-quart [1.9- to 2.8-L]) nonstick sauté pan, warm the oil and garlic over low heat.
2. When the garlic starts to sizzle, add the mint, parsley, and arugula, a pinch of salt, and a grind of black pepper. Cook for 3 minutes on medium heat, stirring constantly so the herbs do not burn.
3. Add the breadcrumbs and stir well. Cook for 4 to 5 minutes, stirring constantly to prevent the breadcrumbs from burning, until the breadcrumbs are uniformly golden brown. Remove from the sauté pan. Sprinkle on soups, salads, and pasta for flavor.

Homemade Breadcrumbs

YIELD: 2 CUPS (216 G) BREADCRUMBS

6 ¼-inch-thick (6-mm-thick) slices crusty white bread

1. Preheat the oven to 250°F (120°C).
2. Place the slices of bread on a baking sheet in a single layer. Bake for 45 to 55 minutes, turning the slices over at a midway point in the baking.
3. Remove the baking sheet from the oven. Let the bread slices cool.
4. Break the slices into smaller pieces and process in a food processor. Use immediately or store in an airtight container for up to 5 days.

Marinated Olives

Olives are a common snack in Sardinia. They also find their way into many dishes, adding flavor and saltiness. The garlic and parsley in this dish give the olives a fresher flavor, balancing their richness.

Serve this appetizer with a glass of chilled Contini Vernaccia di Oristano, which matches the flavors of the olives. For a lighter pairing, try Contini Karmis or Sardus Pater AD49, a sparkling Vermentino with great character.

YIELD: 8–12 SERVINGS

1 pound (454 g) large green olives
4 cloves garlic, thinly sliced
¼ cup (8 g) chopped fresh parsley

1. Combine all the ingredients in a serving bowl. Mix well and refrigerate for at least a couple of hours (and preferably overnight).
2. Serve chilled or at room temperature.

Mini Meatballs

These meatballs are traditionally served at weddings. But whether or not there's a wedding on your agenda, they're an excellent snack, appetizer, or light meal. Freezing the meatballs before cooking ensures that they do not fall apart. The sprinkling of pecorino adds richness, creating a dish that is flavorful, yet light.

Pair the meatballs with a medium-bodied red wine such as Cantina Pili Pujades Monica di Sardegna, an interesting and flavorful red from the monica grape native to Sardinia.

YIELD: 4–8 SERVINGS

FOR THE VEGETABLE STOCK:

- 2 quarts (1.90 L) water
- 1 carrot, peeled and cut into large pieces
- 1 celery rib, cut into large pieces
- 1 small onion, roughly chopped
- 4 stalks parsley, washed

FOR THE MEATBALLS:

- ⅓ pound (151 g) ground veal
- ⅓ pound (151 g) ground pork
- ⅓ pound (151 g) ground chicken
- 1 clove garlic, finely chopped
- 2 tablespoons Homemade Breadcrumbs (see recipe on p. 65)
- 1 tablespoon chopped fresh parsley
- 1 large egg
- ¼ cup (59 mL) milk
- Sea salt and freshly ground black pepper, to taste
- 2 tablespoons freshly grated pecorino, plus more, for sprinkling

TO MAKE THE VEGETABLE STOCK:

1. In a medium (8- to 12-quart [7.6- to 11.4-L]) stockpot, bring the water, carrot, celery, onion, and parsley to a boil.

2. Reduce the heat to low, cover the stockpot, and cook for 30 to 40 minutes.

3. Strain the stock into another bowl or container and discard the vegetables.

Note: The stock can be made up to 2 days ahead and refrigerated. It can also be frozen for up to 2 months.

TO MAKE THE MEATBALLS:

4. In a medium bowl, combine all the ingredients except the pecorino for sprinkling and stir until the mixture is uniform. Let rest for 30 minutes.

5. Make meatballs ½ inch (13 mm) in diameter and place them on a baking sheet. Freeze for at least 2 hours (or overnight).

6. Take the meatballs out of the freezer 5 minutes before cooking. In a medium (8- to 12-quart [7.6- to 11.4-L]) stockpot, warm the Vegetable Stock over medium heat. Once the stock is warmed through, put the frozen meatballs, several at a time, into the stockpot. Boil the meatballs for 7 to 8 minutes, until they are cooked through.

7. With a slotted spoon, take the meatballs out of the stock and place them on a plate lined with paper towels.

8. Transfer the meatballs to a serving platter and serve warm, sprinkled with the remaining pecorino.

Mullet *Bottarga*

Bottarga di muggine, *the pressed, salted, and dried roe of gray mullet, is a Sardinian delicacy. In Sardinia—especially around Cabras and Oristano, on the west coast—*bottarga *is often served thinly sliced as an appetizer. Because* bottarga *has a strong flavor, it is best served with a robust white, such as* Vernaccia di Oristano *or a dry* Malvasia di Bosa. *Another wine that pairs well with sliced* bottarga *is Contini Karmis, a blend of vernaccia and vermentino.*

YIELD: 8–12 SERVINGS

2 ounces (57 g) whole *bottarga*

1. Slice the *bottarga* into paper-thin slices and serve cold or at room temperature.

Octopus in Tomato and Garlic Sauce (*Agliata*)

Agliata is a garlic sauce found in different versions around Italy. It is believed to be of Ligurian origin and likely came to Sardinia during the period when the island was ruled by Genoa. The name of the sauce comes from the Italian word for garlic, aglio, since the sauce has a strong base of garlic. Sardinian *agliata* is unique in that it is made with tomatoes and red wine vinegar. In the past, it was used by fishermen to preserve the catch of the day, especially when it was imperfect and less likely to sell. The fishermen would take agliata with them on the boat; the vinegar and garlic content of the sauce preserved the fish beautifully.

I first tasted *agliata* in one of my favorite restaurants in Sardinia, Trattoria Cavour (now Trattoria Lo Romani) in Alghero. The sauce was tangy and complex, a perfect complement for the boiled octopus. Vittoria, a co-owner of the restaurant, told me that she makes it with both fresh and sundried tomatoes, which explains the richness and depth of flavor. Some Sardinians make it only with fresh or canned tomatoes, but I like the richness the sundried tomatoes give it. *Agliata* can be used as a complement for any fish, but I like to serve it with octopus. The octopus in agliata *pairs perfectly with a high-acid Sardinian* rosato, *such as Argiolas Serra Lori.*

YIELD: 4–6 SERVINGS

- 3 quarts (2.84 L) water
- 1 teaspoon sea salt, plus more, to taste
- 1 pound (454 g) baby octopus*
- 1 tablespoon extra virgin olive oil
- 5 cloves garlic, thinly sliced
- 4 sundried tomatoes, soaked in water for 15 minutes, drained, and chopped
- 1 (14-ounce [397-g]) can whole tomatoes, chopped
- ¼ cup (59 mL) red wine vinegar

1. In a medium (8- to 12-quart [7.6- to 11.4-L]) stockpot, bring to a boil the water and 1 teaspoon of salt. Add the octopus and cook over medium heat for at least 1½ hours, until tender. The octopus should yield easily when pierced with a fork.

2. Drain the octopus and let cool to room temperature. Cut the octopus into bite-sized pieces and set aside.

RECIPE CONTINUES ON PAGE 70

Octopus in Tomato and Garlic Sauce (*Agliata*)

(CONTINUED FROM PAGE 69)

3. In a medium (4- to 5-quart [3.8- to 4.7-L]) sauté pan, warm the oil and garlic over medium-low heat until the garlic starts to sizzle. Add the sundried tomatoes and cook for 2 minutes.
4. Add the canned tomatoes with their juice and cook for 5 to 7 minutes, until the sauce starts to thicken.
5. Raise the heat to medium and add the vinegar. Cook for 2 minutes. Reduce the heat to low and cook for 10 minutes, adjusting the seasoning to taste. Cool to room temperature.
6. In a serving bowl, combine the octopus and sauce, cover tightly with plastic wrap, and chill for at least 2 hours (and up to 2 days). Serve chilled.

*If the octopus is frozen, do not thaw it.

Octopus with Celery

This delicious recipe is inspired by an octopus appetizer at Peschiera Pontis, a fishery outside of Cabras, an area famous for mullet roe and other mullet delicacies. This dish makes an excellent appetizer or a light summer lunch.

Pair this dish with Contini Karmis or Tyrsos Vermentino di Sardegna, two wines from the Cabras area that perfectly complement its flavors.

YIELD: 4 SERVINGS

- 3 quarts (2.84 L) water
- 1 teaspoon sea salt, plus more, to taste
- ½ lemon, sliced
- 1 pound (454 g) octopus*
- 1 celery rib, cut into small cubes
- 3 tablespoons (45 mL) extra virgin olive oil
- 2 tablespoons white wine vinegar

1. In a medium (8- to 12-quart [7.6- to 11.4-L]) stockpot, bring the water, 1 teaspoon of salt, and the lemon slices to a boil. Add the octopus and cook for at least 1½ hours, until tender. The octopus should yield easily when pierced with a fork.
2. Drain and set aside to cool slightly. Cut the octopus into bite-sized pieces.
3. In a serving bowl, combine the octopus, celery, olive oil, and vinegar and stir well. Adjust the seasoning to taste.
4. Refrigerate for at least 4 hours (or overnight). Serve chilled.

*If the octopus is frozen, do not thaw it.

Pane Carasau with Pecorino

Pane carasau, *or music sheet bread, is the traditional bread of Sardinia: paper-thin and crunchy. In this dish, the pecorino melts nicely, giving the cracker-like bread a lot of flavor and saltiness. This is my favorite version of cheese and crackers, because it's very flavorful and makes a perfect snack.*

YIELD: 4–6 SERVINGS

> **4 sheets *pane carasau** (Sardinian music sheet bread)**
> **½ cup (50 g) freshly grated pecorino, for sprinkling**

1. Preheat the oven to 375°F (190°C).
2. Place the sheets of *pane carasau* on a large baking sheet and sprinkle each sheet with pecorino. Toast for 4 minutes, until the pecorino is melted. Remove from the oven.
3. Transfer the *pane carasau* to a serving platter and serve hot.

**Pane carasau is available at Italian groceries, culinary stores, and online from Gourmet Sardinia and Buon Gusto (see p. 260 for contact information).*

Pane Carasau with Olive Oil and Sea Salt (Pane Guttiau)

Pane carasau, *one of the most traditional Sardinian foods, is paper-thin and crispy. Since it lasts a long time, it was eaten by shepherds in the past when they were away from home. To this day,* pane carasau *is served at almost every meal in Sardinia.*

It is often brought to the table toasted and drizzled with flavorful olive oil, which elevates the crispy bread to new heights. The toasting gives the bread a richer flavor, and the olive oil complements the otherwise dry bread perfectly. This remains one of my favorite snacks. I love to surprise guests with this tasty starter, as the combination of the ingredients is amazingly flavorful.

YIELD: 4–6 SERVINGS

- **4 sheets *pane carasau** (Sardinian music sheet bread)**
- **2 tablespoons high-quality extra virgin olive oil (preferably Sardinian)**
- **Sea salt, to taste**

1. Preheat the oven to 375°F (190°C).
2. Place the *pane carasau* on a large baking sheet and toast for 3 to 4 minutes, until golden brown. Remove from the oven.
3. Transfer the bread to a serving platter, drizzle it with the oil, and sprinkle it with the salt. Serve hot or at room temperature.

*Pane carasau *is available at Italian groceries, culinary stores, and online from Gourmet Sardinia and Buon Gusto (see p. 260 for contact information).*

Raw, Fresh Fava with Olive Oil

This dish is perfect as an appetizer or a healthful snack. Fava are full of protein and have a tremendous amount of nutritional value. When they are fresh, they are tender, so a drizzle of high-quality Sardinian olive oil and a sprinkling of salt is all you need for a flavor adventure. This dish pairs well with toasted pane carasau and Cantina di Mogoro Ajò Nuragus di Cagliari.

YIELD: 4–6 SERVINGS

- **2 pounds (908 g) fresh fava, shelled**
- **3–4 tablespoons (45–59 mL) Sardinian olive oil, preferably Montiferru or another spicy variety**
- **Sea salt, to taste**

1. In a serving bowl, toss the fava with the oil and add a sprinkling of salt. Serve at room temperature.

Shrimp Salad

This salad makes a delicious appetizer or a light summer lunch. The fennel and celery add a texture element that complements the shrimp perfectly, and the tomatoes add both acidity and color, tempting the eyes as they do the palate.

Pair the salad with the light and flavorful Argiolas Costamolino.

YIELD: 4 SERVINGS

- **1 pound (454 g) cooked shrimp**
- **1 medium fennel bulb, chopped**
- **1 celery rib, chopped**
- **1 cup (160 g) cherry or grape tomatoes, quartered**
- **¼ cup (59 mL) extra virgin olive oil**
- **¼ cup (59 mL) fresh lemon juice**
- **1½ teaspoons sea salt**

1. In a large serving bowl, combine and toss together the shrimp, fennel, celery, tomatoes, olive oil, lemon juice, and salt.
2. Refrigerate for at least 1 hour (or overnight). Serve chilled.

Steamed Mussels

This easy dish is perfect as an antipasto *or a light summer lunch. For a completely Sardinian experience, pair with Argiolas Serra Lori, a delicious rosato.*

YIELD: 4 SERVINGS

- 1 tablespoon extra virgin olive oil
- 2 cloves garlic, thinly sliced
- ½ celery rib, cut into halves lengthwise and thinly sliced
- 1 pound (454 g) mussels, cleaned and washed
- 1 cup (237 mL) dry white wine
- Sea salt, to taste
- 2 tablespoons finely chopped fresh parsley, for garnish

1. In a large (6- to 7-quart [5.7- to 6.6-L]) sauté pan, warm the oil, garlic, and celery over medium heat.
2. When the garlic and celery start to sizzle, add the mussels, stir, and cook for 2 minutes.
3. Add the wine, stirring well. Cover the pan and cook for 4 to 5 minutes, until the mussels are open. Discard any unopened mussels. Adjust the seasoning to taste.
4. Transfer to a serving bowl and serve hot, garnished with the parsley.

Sweet Pea Frittata

This easy and delicious dish can be an antipasto *or a light meal. It pairs well with a medium-bodied white, such as Argiolas Selegas.*

YIELD: 6–8 SERVINGS

- 3 tablespoons (45 mL) extra virgin olive oil, divided
- ½ medium onion, finely chopped (about ¾ cup [113 g])
- 1 pound (454 g) fresh (or frozen and thawed) sweet peas
- ½ teaspoon sea salt, plus more, to taste
- 3 large eggs

1. In a medium (4- to 5-quart [3.8- to 4.7-L]) sauté pan, warm 2 tablespoons of the oil over medium-low heat. Add the onion and cook for 7 to 8 minutes, until it softens and becomes translucent.
2. Add the peas and ½ teaspoon of salt and cook for at least 20 minutes.
3. Take the pan off the heat. Transfer the peas into a medium bowl, and let cool. Set aside.
4. In a medium bowl, lightly beat the eggs. Add the eggs to the peas and stir well.
5. In a medium cast-iron pan, warm the remaining 1 tablespoon oil over medium heat. Set the oven to broil.
6. Add the pea and egg mixture to the cast-iron pan and cook over low heat for about 15 minutes, until the bottom of the frittata is browned.
7. Finish the frittata under the broiler for 3 to 5 minutes, until the top is browned as well. Remove from the oven.
8. Transfer the frittata to a serving platter, adjust the seasoning to taste, and serve hot.

Tomato Bruschetta with *Bottarga*

Bottarga gives this bruschetta a rich and decadent flavor and also makes it truly Sardinian. Pair with a crisp Sardinian Vermentino *or, even better, Contini Karmis, a blend of vermentino and vernaccia. The richness of Karmis matches the* bottarga *perfectly.*

YIELD: 4 SERVINGS

- 1 large ripe tomato, chopped
- 2 tablespoons extra virgin olive oil
- Sea salt, to taste
- 2 slices crusty bread, cut into halves
- 1 teaspoon grated *bottarga*

1. In a small bowl, combine the tomato, oil, and salt. Stir well and set aside.
2. Toast the bread.
3. Place the bread on a serving platter. Distribute the tomato mixture evenly atop the 4 pieces of bread and sprinkle with the *bottarga*. Serve immediately.

Vegetable Fritters

Roberto Flore, the talented chef at Antica Dimora del Gruccione, a family-owned hotel and restaurant, showed me how to make these fritters, which are one of my favorite appetizers. When I am fortunate enough to have dinner at Antica Dimora del Gruccione, I anxiously anticipate Roberto's fritters. They are seasonal, and the ingredients change depending on what is locally available. But no matter what greens Roberto uses, the fritters never disappoint.

Pair with Sardus Pater AD49. This unique bubbly is a perfect match for the crisp and rich fritters.

YIELD: 4 SERVINGS

- 2 cups (260 g) finely chopped seasonal green vegetables (wild fennel or fennel greens, asparagus, zucchini, etc.)
- 2 large eggs, lightly beaten
- ½ cup (119 mL) extra virgin olive oil
- 1⅓ cups (167 g) all-purpose flour
- Sea salt, to taste
- 1 quart (948 mL) frying oil*

1. In a mixing bowl, combine the greens, eggs, olive oil, flour, and salt. Stir well. The dough should be thick.
2. In a deep frying pan or a Dutch oven, heat the oil. Spoon the dough into the hot oil and cook the fritters for 2 to 3 minutes per side, until they are golden brown. Remove from the oil and place on paper towels to absorb the excess oil.
3. Transfer the fritters to a serving bowl or platter and serve hot.

I use extra virgin olive oil for frying these fritters, but Roberto prefers the lighter flavor of peanut oil. If you use extra virgin olive oil, keep in mind that it smokes at a lower temperature than peanut oil, so be careful not to burn it.

Vegetable *Panada*

Sardinia has a strong tradition of panadas, pies filled with anything from meat and fish to a variety of vegetables. This versatile dish is great as an appetizer, as party fare, or as a full meal. Pair this rich vegetable starter with Argiolas Perdera, a light and flavorful red made from Sardinia's native monica grape.

YIELD: 6–8 SERVINGS

FOR THE DOUGH:

- 3 cups (375 g) all-purpose flour
- ½ teaspoon sea salt
- 2 tablespoons chilled butter, cubed
- 2 cups (474 mL) lukewarm water, as needed

FOR THE VEGETABLES:

- 1 small eggplant, cubed (about 4 cups [328 g])
- 1 quart (948 mL) water
- ½ teaspoon sea salt, plus more, for the eggplant and to taste
- ½ pound (227 g) green beans, cut into ½-inch (13-mm) pieces
- ¼ cup (59 mL) extra virgin olive oil, plus more, for brushing
- 1 large potato, cubed
- 1 carrot, roughly chopped
- 1 celery rib, roughly chopped
- 1 red onion, roughly chopped
- 1 medium zucchini, roughly chopped
- 1 cup (145 g) fresh (or frozen and thawed) peas
- 2 sundried tomatoes, chopped
- 1 large egg yolk, for brushing

TO MAKE THE DOUGH:

1. In a bowl or on a flat working surface, arrange the flour in a mound. Sprinkle with the salt. Make a crater in the center of the mound and place the butter inside. Add a little water and start incorporating the butter and water into the flour. Slowly continue to add the water until the dough is soft, but not sticky, and can be worked. Knead for 5 minutes, until the dough is smooth.
2. Wrap the dough in plastic wrap and let rest on the kitchen counter for at least 30 minutes.

TO MAKE THE VEGETABLES:

3. Place the cubes of eggplant into a colander. Sprinkle them with salt and cover them with a small plate weighed down with a heavy object (such as a large can of tomatoes). Let the eggplant sit for at least 20 minutes with the plate pressing down on it. Rinse the eggplant with cold water and set aside.
4. In a medium (8- to 12-quart [7.6- to 11.4-L]) stockpot, bring the water to a boil. Add ½ teaspoon of salt and the green beans and cook for 2 to 3 minutes. Remove from the heat. Drain and set aside.
5. In a large (6- to 7-quart [5.7- to 6.6-L]) sauté pan, warm the oil. Add the eggplant, potato, carrot, celery, onion, and zucchini, and cook for 12 to 15 minutes. Add the peas, sundried tomatoes, and green beans, and cook for 2 to 3 minutes, until the flavors have blended. Adjust the seasoning to taste.

TO MAKE THE *PANADA*:

6. Preheat the oven to 375°F (190°C).
7. Divide the dough into 2 unequal parts: 1 about ⅔ of the total, the other ⅓ of the total. Roll out each piece of dough to a ¼-inch (6-mm) thickness.
8. Brush a 13-inch (32.5-cm) round baking dish with the oil. Place the larger piece of dough on the bottom of the dish and let it fall over the sides.
9. Place the vegetables in the dough shell, distributing them evenly. Cover the vegetables with the smaller piece of dough and pinch the 2 layers together to close the *Panada*.
10. Cut off any excess dough.
11. Brush the top of the *Panada* with the egg yolk and bake for 30 to 40 minutes. Remove from the oven.
12. Serve the *Panada* in the baking dish either hot or at room temperature.

Primi

SARDINIA'S *PRIMI* (FIRST COURSES) ARE almost as varied and fascinating as its *antipasti*. From unique and unusual pastas to soups of every persuasion, the island displays its bounty in interesting first courses that creatively combine local ingredients and showcase typical flavors.

PASTA AND RISOTTO

Sardinia has some of the most varied and interesting types of pasta. A few of the pasta shapes are unique to the island and have a long history.

The two most typical shapes are *malloreddus*, also known as *gnocchetti sardi*, and *fregola*. *Fregola* is best described as a cross between pasta and couscous, which speaks to how varied the influences are that shaped Sardinian cuisine. *Fregola* is versatile, too—it can stand alone as a pasta dish, but it is also often used to thicken soups.

The list of uniquely Sardinian pasta also includes: *macarrones de busa*, shaped by wrapping pasta strands around bicycle spokes; *lorighitas*, hoop-shaped pasta still made by hand in the small village of Morgongiori; and *filindeu*, thin, hand-pulled strands of pasta.

Sardinia also offers many types of filled pastas. *Culurgiones* are ravioli filled either with potatoes and mint (this is the variety most commonly found in the province of Ogliastra) or ricotta and greens. Sardinian cooks take great pride in their ravioli; each part of the island has its own unique recipes with local ingredients.

So, when you travel to Sardinia, make sure to explore its pasta creations. Not only will you have a great meal, but you'll learn interesting facts about the history of the island, simply by studying the pasta on your plate!

Baked *Fregola* with Pecorino

This recipe is the essence of Sardinia: Fregola *and two types of pecorino combine in a rich, satisfying dish that warms you up on a cold winter day. This dish is perfect as a light meal or as the opening of a more elaborate meal that includes simple roasted meats and vegetables. Pair this dish with a full-bodied white, such as Argiolas Is Argiolas.*

YIELD: 8 SERVINGS

- 1 quart (948 mL) Vegetable Stock (see recipe in the Mini Meatballs recipe on page 66)
- 2 tablespoons extra virgin olive oil
- ½ small onion, finely chopped (about ½ cup [75 g])
- 1⅓ cups (253 g) large *fregola**
- ½ teaspoon sea salt, plus more, to taste
- 1½ cups (150 g) freshly grated young pecorino, for sprinkling
- ¾ cup (75 g) freshly grated aged pecorino (such as Academia Barilla Pecorino Gran Cru), for sprinkling

1. Preheat the oven to 400°F (200°C).
2. In a small (3- to 4-quart [2.8- to 3.8-L]) stockpot, warm the Vegetable Stock over medium-low heat.
3. In a Dutch oven, warm the oil. Add the onion and cook for 7 to 8 minutes, until it softens and becomes translucent.
4. Add the *fregola*, stir well, and cook for 1 minute.
5. Add the Vegetable Stock and ½ teaspoon salt to the Dutch oven. Bring to a boil and cook for 10 to 12 minutes, until the *fregola* is al dente.
6. Distribute half of the young pecorino on the bottom of a 9 × 9-inch (22.5 × 22.5-cm) baking dish.
7. Pour the *fregola* and its cooking liquid over the pecorino. Sprinkle on the remaining young and the aged pecorino. Adjust the seasoning to taste.
8. Bake for at least 15 minutes, until the top is brown and the cheese has melted. Remove from the oven.
9. Serve hot in the baking dish.

*Fregola *is available at culinary stores and online from Gourmet Sardinia (see p. 260 for contact information).*

Baked Semolina Gnocchi with Meat Sauce

This is the perfect comfort dish, especially on a cold day. It makes a great weekend dinner and any leftovers reheat well. The tomato sauce makes it zesty and delicious, and the semolina gnocchi make the perfect base for the full-bodied sauce.

Serve with a robust red wine, such as Cantina Oliena Nepente di Oliena.

YIELD: 6 SERVINGS

FOR THE GNOCCHI:
- 1 quart (948 mL) 1% milk
- 1½ cups (334 g) semolina flour
- 2 large egg yolks
- ¼ cup (25 g) freshly grated pecorino
- Sea salt, to taste

FOR THE TOMATO SAUCE:
- 2 tablespoons extra virgin olive oil
- 4 cloves garlic, minced
- 1 (28-ounce [784-g]) can whole tomatoes (preferably San Marzano), chopped
- Sea salt, to taste

FOR THE MEAT SAUCE:
- 1 tablespoon extra virgin olive oil
- ⅓ cup (50 g) chopped pancetta
- ½ medium onion, chopped
- ¼ pound (114 g) ground pork
- ¼ pound (114 g) ground beef
- 1 cup (237 mL) dry white wine
- Sea salt, to taste

FOR THE ASSEMBLED DISH:
- 2 tablespoons extra virgin olive oil, for greasing
- ¾ cup (75 g) freshly grated pecorino, for sprinkling

TO MAKE THE GNOCCHI:

1. In a large (4- to 5-quart [3.8- to 4.7-L]) saucepan, bring the milk to a boil over medium-high heat. Slowly pour in the semolina flour, stirring constantly with a whisk to break up any lumps. Reduce the heat to low and continue cooking for 10 minutes, stirring constantly to prevent the semolina from sticking to the bottom. Remove the pan from the heat and let cool for 1 to 2 minutes.

2. Add the egg yolks and stir until they are fully incorporated into the mixture. Add the pecorino and mix well. Adjust the seasoning to taste.

3. Pour the mixture out onto a large cutting board or a large dish (12 inches [30 cm] minimum). Spread the mixture with a spatula to make sure it is of uniform thickness throughout. Let cool for several minutes and cut into 1-inch (2.5-cm) squares. Set aside.

TO MAKE THE TOMATO SAUCE:

4. In a medium (4- to 5-quart [3.8- to 4.7-L]) sauté pan, heat the oil and garlic over low heat.

5. When the garlic starts to sizzle, add the tomatoes and their juice and cook on low heat for 15 to 20 minutes, until the sauce thickens. Adjust the seasoning to taste. Remove from the heat and set aside.

TO MAKE THE MEAT SAUCE:

6. In a large (6- to 7-quart [5.7- to 6.6-L]) sauté pan, warm the oil over medium heat. Add the pancetta and cook for 2 minutes, until its fat starts to melt.

7. Add the onion and cook for 7 to 8 minutes, until it softens and becomes translucent.

8. Add the ground pork and beef. Raise the heat to medium-high and cook for 5 to 7 minutes, until the meat is browned, breaking up any lumps with a wooden spoon.

9. Add the wine and cook until the alcohol has evaporated and the liquid has reduced by about ½. Adjust the seasoning to taste.

TO ASSEMBLE THE DISH:

10. Preheat the oven to 375°F (190°C).

11. Grease a 9 × 12-inch (22.5 × 30-cm) baking dish with the oil. Spread a ladleful of the tomato sauce and ½ cup (119 mL) of the meat sauce on the bottom of the dish. Cover with 1 layer of gnocchi squares. Continue to layer, finishing with a layer of gnocchi. Sprinkle generously with the pecorino.

12. Bake for 40 minutes, until the pecorino is melted and forms a crust. Remove from the oven.

13. Serve hot in the baking dish.

Corkscrew-Shaped Pasta with Zucchini Cream and *Bottarga*

This is one of my favorite comfort dishes: It's light but flavorful, and perfect for summer. The bottarga *adds complexity and character, enriching the silky zucchini sauce.*

This is also the perfect dish for entertaining. The sauce can be made ahead of time, so you can chat with your guests without having to spend too much time in the kitchen. Pair this dish with Contini Karmis.

YIELD: 4 SERVINGS

FOR THE ZUCCHINI CREAM:

- 2 tablespoons extra virgin olive oil
- 1 medium onion, chopped
- 3 medium zucchini, cut into quarters lengthwise and then sliced
- ⅔ teaspoon sea salt
- 1 cup (237 mL) Vegetable Stock (see recipe in the Mini Meatballs recipe on page 66), plus more, as needed

FOR THE PASTA:

- 1 gallon (3.80 L) water
- 1 tablespoon sea salt
- 4 cups (11 ounces [312 g]) *celentani* (corkscrew-shaped) or fusilli
- 2 teaspoons grated *bottarga,* for sprinkling

TO MAKE THE ZUCCHINI CREAM:

1. In a large (6- to 7-quart [5.7- to 6.6-L]) sauté pan, warm the oil over medium-low heat. Add the onion and cook for 4 to 5 minutes, until it starts to soften.
2. Add the zucchini, ⅔ teaspoon of salt, and the Vegetable Stock. Stir well and bring to a boil. Cover the sauté pan and cook for 10 minutes. If the zucchini dry out completely, add a little more Vegetable Stock or water.
3. When the zucchini are softened, remove the sauté pan from the heat and let the zucchini cool a little.
4. Transfer the zucchini to a food processor or blender and process to a creamy, thick, and uniform consistency. (The Zucchini Cream can be made up to 2 days in advance and refrigerated in an airtight container.)

TO MAKE THE PASTA:

5. In a medium (8- to 10-quart [7.6- to 9.5-L]) stockpot, boil the water and 1 tablespoon of salt. Add the pasta and cook until it is almost al dente, 1 minute less than the package instructions.
6. Drain the pasta, reserving 1 cup (237 mL) of the cooking water.
7. In a large (6- to 7-quart [5.7- to 6.6-L]) sauté pan, warm the Zucchini Cream. If necessary, add a little of the reserved cooking water. Add the pasta and toss well to combine.
8. Transfer the dressed pasta to a serving bowl and sprinkle with the *bottarga*. Serve hot.

Couscous with Vegetables

The tiny island of San Pietro, off the southwest coast of Sardinia, is a true blend of traditions. A 30-minute boat ride from Sardinia, this tiny Mediterranean outpost is the least Sardinian of all places. It is a mix of Ligurian and North African influences, both culturally and in terms of cuisine. Couscous is a popular dish here, and it is prepared in many different ways. This version, which is vegetarian, is often served almost at room temperature, especially in the summer.

For a perfect meal, pair this dish with Argiolas Iselis Bianco, a light yet flavorful blend of nasco, a uniquely Sardinian white grape, and vermentino.

YIELD: 8 SERVINGS

- 1 cup (227 g) dry garbanzo beans (chickpeas), soaked overnight in cold water
- 2 whole cloves garlic, divided
- 2½ teaspoons sea salt, divided
- 7 tablespoons (105 mL) extra virgin olive oil, divided
- 1 small onion, chopped
- ½ teaspoon crushed red pepper
- 4 ripe tomatoes, chopped
- 1 zucchini, cut in half lengthwise and sliced into ¼-inch (6-mm) slices
- 1 medium carrot, cut in half lengthwise and sliced into ¼-inch (6-mm) slices
- ½ small head cauliflower, cubed (about 1½ cups [150 g])
- 1½ cups (105 g) shredded green cabbage
- 4 cups (948 mL) water, divided
- 1 small eggplant, cubed
- 2 cups (346 g) whole wheat couscous

1. In a medium (8- to 12-quart [7.6- to 11.4-L]) stockpot, cover the garbanzo beans with cold water to about 1 inch (2.5 cm) above the beans. Add 1 clove of the garlic and 1 teaspoon of salt. Bring to a boil. Reduce the heat to medium-low and cook the beans for at least 1½ hours, or until they are thoroughly cooked. Remove from the heat. Drain and set aside.
2. In a Dutch oven, warm 3 tablespoons (45 mL) of the oil over medium heat. Add the onion and cook for 7 to 8 minutes, until it softens and becomes translucent.
3. Add the remaining garlic clove, crushed red pepper, and cloves and continue cooking for 1 minute.

4. Add the tomatoes, zucchini, carrot, cauliflower, cabbage, 2 cups of the water, and ½ teaspoon of salt. Bring to a boil. Reduce the heat to low and cook for 15 to 20 minutes. Remove from the heat.

5. In a large (6- to 7-quart [5.7- to 6.6-L]) nonstick sauté pan, warm 3 tablespoons (45 mL) of the oil over medium-high heat. Add the eggplant and cook until it is browned on all sides. With a slotted spoon, transfer the eggplant to a serving platter lined with paper towels.

6. In a medium (8- to 12-quart [7.6- to 11.4-L]) stockpot, bring the remaining 2 cups of water, remaining 1 tablespoon (15 mL) of oil, and remaining 1 teaspoon of salt to a boil. Add the couscous and stir well. Remove from the heat, cover, and let it sit for 5 minutes.

7. In a large serving bowl, combine the couscous with the stewed vegetables, fried eggplant, and garbanzo beans. Stir well. Serve hot or lukewarm.

Fettuccine with Olives, Capers, and Tuna

This recipe was inspired by a dish I fell in love with on the island of San Pietro. On one windy April day, we took the ferry from Sant'Antioco to Carloforte to taste some of the island's world-famous tuna. Alas, it was too early in the year for fresh tuna, but we did have excellent tuna packed in oil. San Pietro tuna is of high quality and tastes fresh even when preserved in oil. For this dish, use the best oil-packed tuna you can find, as the tuna is the star of the show.

Pair with Sardus Pater Horus, a rosato of unique flavor and complexity.

YIELD: 4 SERVINGS

- 2 tablespoons extra virgin olive oil
- ½ cup (67 g) green olives, chopped
- ½ cup (67 g) black olives, chopped
- 2 tablespoons salt-packed capers, rinsed and roughly chopped
- 1 (5-ounce [142-g]) can tuna packed in oil, drained
- 1 gallon (3.80 L) water
- 1 tablespoon sea salt, plus more, to taste
- 11 ounces (312 g) fettuccine, preferably fresh*

1. In a large (6- to 7-quart [5.7- to 6.6-L]) sauté pan, warm the oil over medium heat. Add the olives and capers and cook for 2 minutes, stirring occasionally.
2. Add the tuna, stir well, and cook for 1 minute. Remove from the heat and set aside.
3. In a medium (8- to 12-quart [7.6- to 11.4-L]) stockpot, bring the water and 1 tablespoon of salt to a boil. Add the fettuccine and cook until almost al dente, 1 minute less than the time indicated on the package. Remove from the heat. Drain the fettuccine, reserving 2 cups (474 mL) of the cooking liquid, and transfer the pasta back into the pot.
4. Add the olive, caper, and tuna sauce to the pot and toss well to combine, adding enough of the reserved cooking water to create a thick sauce that will bind the pasta, tuna, olives, and capers. Cook over medium heat for 1 minute for the flavors to blend. Adjust the seasoning to taste. Transfer to a serving bowl and serve hot.

*Fresh fettuccine are available in specialized fresh pasta shops and in many grocery stores.

Fregola with Clams

This is a very traditional Sardinian dish, especially in the southern part of the island. It is the essence of Sardinia as it uses fregola, *the most unique Sardinian pasta, and* arselle, *the small clams you find on every menu in southern Sardinia. The dish can be made with mussels or shrimp, if you prefer, but the most traditional version features clams.*

Pair with the crisp and refreshing Argiolas Costamolino, a great everyday Vermentino *that is quite versatile with food.*

YIELD: 4 SERVINGS

- 2 tablespoons extra virgin olive oil
- 1 whole clove garlic
- 1 (28-ounce [784-g]) can whole tomatoes, chopped
- ½ teaspoon crushed red pepper
- 1–1½ pounds (454–681 g) clams, washed
- 1½ cups (285 g) medium *fregola**
- Sea salt, to taste
- 2 tablespoons chopped fresh parsley

1. In a large (6- to 7-quart [5.7- to 6.6-L]) sauté pan, warm the oil and garlic over medium-low heat. When the garlic starts to sizzle, add the tomatoes and crushed red pepper. Stir and cook for 5 to 6 minutes, until the sauce starts to thicken.

2. In another large (6- to 7-quart [5.7- to 6.6-L]) sauté pan, place the clams over medium heat. Cover the sauté pan and cook for 3 to 5 minutes, until the clams open. Discard any unopened clams. Remove from the heat. Drain the water released by the clams through a sieve and reserve it. Set the clams aside.

3. Add the *fregola* and reserved clam water to the tomato sauce. Stir well and continue cooking until the *fregola* is al dente, following the package instructions. When the *fregola* is done, remove the garlic clove. Stir well. If the *fregola* is too dry, add more water. (The dish should have the consistency of risotto.)

4. Season with salt to taste. Be sure to adjust the seasoning to taste only after you have added all the clam water, which contains a fair amount of salt.

5. To the sauté pan containing the *fregola*, add the clams. Stir well, and cook for 1 minute, until the clams warm through and the flavors blend. Transfer to a serving bowl and serve hot, sprinkled with the parsley.

**Fregola is available at culinary stores and online from Gourmet Sardinia (see p. 260 for contact information).*

Fregola with Sausage and Pecorino

In cooler weather, this is the perfect soul-warming dish. It speaks of Sardinia because it includes some of the most traditional Sardinian ingredients: fregola, sausage, and pecorino.

Pair with a robust red, such as Sardus Pater Is Solus Carignano del Sulcis.

YIELD: 6 SERVINGS

- 3 tablespoons (45 mL) extra virgin olive oil
- ½ small onion, chopped
- ½ celery rib, chopped
- 1 small carrot, chopped
- 1 clove garlic, thinly sliced
- ½ pound (227 g) mild Italian sausage, casings removed
- 2 cups (380 g) medium *fregola**
- 1 cup (100 g) cubed young pecorino
- ½ cup (50 g) freshly grated aged pecorino
- 1 quart (948 mL) beef or lamb broth
- Sea salt, to taste

1. Preheat the oven to 350°F (180°C).
2. In a large (6- to 7-quart [5.7- to 6.6-L]) sauté pan, warm the oil over medium heat. Add the onion, celery, and carrot. Stir well and cook for 5 to 6 minutes, until the onion and vegetables start to soften.
3. Add the garlic and cook for 1 minute.
4. Add the sausage, breaking it up with a wooden spoon, and continue cooking for 6 to 7 minutes, until the sausage is browned.
5. Add the *fregola* and a pinch of salt or more to taste. Stir well, and cook for 1 to 2 minutes. Remove the sauté pan from the heat.
6. Add the young and aged pecorino and stir well.
7. Transfer to a 9 × 9-inch (22.5 × 22.5-cm) baking dish. Add the meat broth and stir well.
8. Bake for 40 minutes. Remove from the oven.
9. Serve hot in the baking dish.

*Fregola *is available at culinary stores and online from Gourmet Sardinia (see p. 260 for contact information).

Lasagne with Tuna and Pesto

This recipe was inspired by some heavenly lasagne we enjoyed at Da Andrea in Carloforte. In my wildest dreams, I could not have imagined tuna featured this way. The Béchamel Sauce provides the perfect background for the tuna and Fresh Pesto, two strong flavors that work in harmony in each delicious bite. I make Béchamel Sauce with extra virgin olive oil, so it's a little lighter and matches the weight of the tuna better. Pair with a flavorful rosato, *such as Sardus Pater Horus, or Sardus Pater AD49, a unique sparkling* Vermentino *made in the traditional method.*

YIELD: 4 SERVINGS

FOR THE FRESH PASTA:*
 1½ cups (188 g) all-purpose flour
 2 large eggs
 Sea salt, to taste
 Cold water, as needed

FOR THE PESTO:
 3 cups (72 g) fresh basil leaves, washed and patted dry
 1 tablespoon toasted pine nuts
 3 tablespoons (45 mL) extra virgin olive oil
 Sea salt, to taste

FOR THE BÉCHAMEL SAUCE:
 5 tablespoons (74 mL) extra virgin olive oil
 ¼ cup (31 g) all-purpose flour
 3 cups (711 mL) skim or 1% milk
 Sea salt, to taste

FOR THE LASAGNE:
 ¼ cup (59 mL) Fresh Pesto
 1 (5-ounce [142-g]) can oil-packed tuna, drained

TO MAKE THE FRESH PASTA:

1. Combine the flour, eggs, and a pinch of salt in a large bowl. Stir with a fork, adding a little cold water, as necessary.
2. When the dough comes together, take it out of the bowl and knead it on a clean working surface for at least 10 minutes. The dough should be smooth and elastic.
3. Wrap the dough in plastic wrap and refrigerate for at least 20 minutes. (The dough can be made 1 day ahead and refrigerated overnight.)
4. Roll out the dough to 1/16-inch (1.6-mm) thickness. Cut it into 2-inch- (5-cm-) wide strips. Set aside.

TO MAKE THE PESTO:

5. In the bowl of a food processor, combine all the ingredients. Process thoroughly.
6. Adjust the seasoning to taste. Use immediately or refrigerate.

TO MAKE THE BÉCHAMEL SAUCE:

7. In a large (4- to 5-quart [3.8- to 4.7-L]) saucepan, warm the oil over medium heat. Slowly add the flour, whisking to break up any lumps. Cook for 4 to 5 minutes, whisking constantly.
8. In the meantime, in a small (1-quart [948-mL]) saucepan, warm the milk. Add the milk to the flour and oil mixture, 1 ladle at a time, whisking constantly to combine.
9. Continue cooking for 6 to 7 minutes, whisking constantly, until the Béchamel Sauce starts to thicken. Season with the salt to taste.
10. Set aside to cool. (The Béchamel Sauce can be made several hours ahead and refrigerated until ready to use.)

TO ASSEMBLE THE LASAGNE:

11. Preheat the oven to 375°F (190°C).
12. In a 9 × 12-inch (22.5 × 30-cm) baking dish, spread ½ cup (119 mL) of the Béchamel Sauce. Line the bottom of the dish with the pasta sheets. Crumble ⅓ of the tuna on top of the pasta.
13. Sprinkle the tuna with 1 tablespoon of the Fresh Pesto and evenly spread on top 1 cup (237 mL) of the Béchamel Sauce. Continue the layering process, finishing with the Béchamel Sauce.
14. Bake for 1 hour, or until the top is golden brown. Remove from the oven.
15. Serve hot in the baking dish.

I always make lasagne with fresh pasta, but you can substitute dry pasta. Simply follow the package instructions.

Linguine with Lobster

This dish was inspired by one of my all-time Sardinian favorites at the former Trattoria Cavour (now Trattoria Lo Romani) in Alghero: linguine with scampi. Scampi, which are also known as *langoustines* or small lobsters, are close in flavor to lobster and crayfish. In the U.S., the term *scampi* is often used to indicate not an ingredient but a type of preparation—usually shrimp cooked in garlic, butter, and white wine. In this recipe, it refers to the ingredient. Scampi are difficult to find, so I suggest using lobster or crayfish. Shrimp or prawns are very different in flavor, and substituting one for the other changes the dish.

Pair with Contini Karmis or Argiolas Serra Lori rosato.

YIELD: 4 SERVINGS

- 3 tablespoons (45 mL) extra virgin olive oil
- 2 cloves garlic, thinly sliced
- ½ tablespoon minced fresh parsley
- 1 pound (454 g) lobster tail, cut into ½-inch (13-mm) pieces
- 1 cup (237 mL) dry white wine
- 1 tablespoon tomato paste
- ½ teaspoon crushed red pepper (optional)
- 2 fresh bay leaves
- 1 gallon (3.80 L) water
- 1 tablespoon sea salt, plus more, to taste
- 11 ounces (312 g) linguine

1. In a medium (4- to 5-quart [3.8- to 4.7-L]) sauté pan, warm the oil and garlic over medium-low heat until the garlic starts to sizzle.
2. Add the parsley and cook for 1 minute. Add the lobster and toss. Cook for 1 minute.
3. Add the wine. Turn up the heat to medium-high and cook for 2 minutes, until the alcohol in the wine has evaporated.
4. Add the tomato paste and crushed red pepper (if using) and cook for 1 minute, until the tomato paste dissolves.
5. Add the bay leaves and stir. Reduce the heat to low and cook for 20 to 25 minutes, until the lobster is cooked through.

6. Meanwhile, in a medium (8- to 12-quart [7.6- to 11.4-L]) stockpot, bring the water and 1 tablespoon salt to a boil. Add the pasta and cook until it is almost al dente, 1 minute less than the package instructions. Drain the pasta, reserving 1 cup (237 mL) of the cooking water.

7. Remove and discard the bay leaves from the lobster sauce. Toss the linguine with the lobster sauce and cook for an additional 30 seconds, adding some of the reserved cooking water if necessary to bring the sauce to the desired consistency. Adjust the seasoning to taste. Transfer the pasta to a serving bowl. Serve hot.

Lorighitas with Free-Range Chicken Sauce

Free-range chicken has a firmer texture than regular chicken, which makes it perfect for this slow-cooked sauce. It also has a lot of flavor, which intensifies during the cooking process. In Sardinia, this is one of the traditional sauces for lorighitas, *a thick pasta that can stand up to more robust sauces.* Lorighitas *is very difficult to find in the United States, so you can substitute other short, thick pasta, such as strozzapreti, gemelli, and even rigatoni.*

Pair with a medium-bodied red wine, such as Cantina Pili Pujades Monica di Sardegna.

YIELD: 6 SERVINGS

- 2 tablespoons extra virgin olive oil
- ½ yellow onion, chopped
- 1 clove garlic, thinly sliced
- 1 tablespoon chopped fresh parsley
- ½ free-range chicken, cut into several pieces
- 1 cup (237 mL) dry white wine
- 2 cups (320 g) chopped tomatoes (fresh or canned)
- Pinch saffron
- 1 tablespoon sea salt, plus more, to taste
- Freshly ground black pepper, to taste
- 1 gallon (3.80 L) water
- 4 cups (12 ounces [341 g]) *lorighitas*, gemelli, or strozzapreti
- ½ cup (50 g) freshly grated pecorino, for sprinkling

1. In a large (6- to 7-quart [5.7- to 6.6-L]) sauté pan, warm the oil over medium heat. Add the onion and cook for 7 to 8 minutes, until it softens and becomes translucent. Add the garlic and parsley, stir well, and cook for 1 minute.
2. Add the chicken. Stir well and cook for 7 to 8 minutes, until the chicken is browned on all sides.
3. Add the wine and cook for 2 minutes. Cover the sauté pan. Reduce the heat to low and cook for 10 minutes, adding a little warm water if the dish dries out.
4. Add the tomatoes, saffron, and some salt and black pepper, stir well, and cook, covered, on low heat for 25 minutes, until the meat is tender and falls apart. If necessary, add some water during the cooking. Remove from the heat.

5. Remove the meat from the bones and discard the bones. Return the meat to the sauce and set aside."

6. In a medium (8- to 12-quart [7.6- to 11.4-L]) stockpot, bring the water and 1 tablespoon salt to a boil. Add the pasta and cook until almost al dente, 1 minute less than the package instructions.

7. Drain the pasta, reserving 1 cup (237 mL) of the cooking water.

8. Toss the pasta with the sauce, adding some of the reserved cooking water, if necessary. Stir well and continue cooking for 1 minute or so, until the flavors blend. Adjust the seasoning to taste.

9. Transfer the pasta to a serving bowl. Serve hot, sprinkled with the pecorino.

Malloreddus (Gnocchetti Sardi)

Malloreddus, *or* gnocchetti sardi, *is one of the island's most traditional pasta shapes. I learned the intricacies of* malloreddus *at Su Barchile in Orosei, with Signora Maria Teresa by my side. The Signora guided me and showed me her secrets to the perfect* malloreddus.

Malloreddus *is easy to make and requires no special tools; a fork or grater will do just fine. Making the pasta at home is relaxing and fun—it's an activity that even kids can participate in. Making* Malloreddus *is more an art than a science, so relax and play with your food! You will love the fruits of your labor.*

◊◊◊

YIELD: 3 CUPS (11 OUNCES [312 G])

2 cups (280 g) *semola rimacinata**
Sea salt, to taste
¾ cup (178 mL) lukewarm water, plus more, as needed

1. In a bowl or on a flat working surface, create a mound with the *semola rimacinata* and make a well in the center. Add a pinch of salt. Very slowly, start adding the water, stirring with a fork to incorporate it into the *semola rimacinata*. Continue adding the water, a little at a time, until the dough comes together but is not sticky. If the dough sticks to your hands, add more *semola rimacinata*. If the dough is too dry, add a little more water.

2. Knead the dough for about 10 minutes. Shape it into a ball, cover it with plastic wrap, and let it rest for at least 20 minutes.

3. Divide the dough into 8 balls. Roll each ball into a snakelike shape, about ½ inch (13 mm) in diameter. Cut each dough snake into ½-inch (13-mm) pieces. Roll the pieces off the reverse side of a cheese grater or off a fork to give each piece the *malloreddus* texture.

Storage Note: Malloreddus *can be refrigerated overnight or frozen for up to 1 month. Do not thaw frozen* Malloreddus *before cooking. Simply add the frozen pasta to boiling salted water.*

*Semola rimacinata *is finely ground semolina (durum wheat) flour. If you cannot find* semola rimacinata, *use ½ regular semolina flour and ½ all-purpose flour.*

Malloreddus with Fresh Fava and Pecorino

This is the perfect spring dish: Fresh fava have a tantalizingly fresh yet meaty flavor, and the young pecorino is mild enough not to cover up that flavor. Use young pecorino, as it melts well. This dish pairs well with a young and fresh Vermentino di Sardegna, *such as Sardus Pater Terre Fenicie.*

YIELD: 4 SERVINGS

- 3 tablespoons (45 mL) extra virgin olive oil
- 2 cups (300 g) shelled fresh fava
- 1 tablespoon sea salt, plus more, to taste
- 1 gallon (3.80 L) water
- 3 cups (312 g) fresh *Malloreddus* (see recipe on p. 110) or other short pasta, such as shells or elbows
- ¾ cup (75 g) freshly grated pecorino, for sprinkling

1. In a large (6- to 7-quart [5.7- to 6.6-L]) sauté pan, warm the oil and add the fava. Cook for 5 to 6 minutes, until the fava start to soften. Add a pinch of salt. Remove from the heat. Set aside.
2. In a medium (8- to 12-quart [7.6- to 11.4-L]) stockpot, bring the water and 1 tablespoon salt to a boil. Add the *Malloreddus* and cook for 3 to 5 minutes, until the pasta is almost al dente. (If you are using dry pasta, follow the package instructions.) Remove from the heat.
3. Drain the *Malloreddus*, reserving 1 cup (237 mL) of the cooking water.
4. Toss the *Malloreddus* with the fava and stir well, adding ½ cup (119 mL) of the reserved cooking water to create a sauce. Cook for 1 minute or so, until the flavors blend.
5. Transfer the *Malloreddus* and fava to a serving bowl. Serve hot, sprinkled with the pecorino.

Malloreddus with Meat Sauce

This is the Sardinian version of pasta with meat sauce. This pasta shape is traditionally Sardinian and the meat sauce contains lamb, a common Sardinian ingredient. For a perfect dinner, pair this dish with a medium-bodied red, such as Cantina Pili Pujades Monica di Sardegna.

YIELD: 4–6 SERVINGS

- 2 tablespoons extra virgin olive oil
- ½ medium carrot, peeled and finely chopped
- ½ celery rib, finely chopped
- ½ medium onion, finely chopped
- 1 clove garlic, thinly sliced
- 1 bay leaf
- ½ pound (227 g) ground lamb
- ½ pound (227 g) ground pork
- 1 cup (237 mL) dry white wine
- 1 (14-ounce [397-g]) can whole tomatoes, chopped
- 1 tablespoon sea salt, plus more, to taste
- Freshly ground black pepper, to taste
- 1 gallon (3.80 L) water
- 3 cups (312 g) fresh *Malloreddus* (see recipe on p. 110) or other short pasta, such as shells or elbows
- ¼ cup (25 g) freshly grated pecorino, for sprinkling

1. In a large (6- to 7-quart [5.7- to 6.6-L]) sauté pan or Dutch oven, warm the oil over medium heat. Add the carrots, celery, and onion and cook for 5 minutes, until the vegetables start to soften.
2. Add the garlic and bay leaf. Stir well and cook for 1 minute.
3. Add the lamb and pork. Stir well and cook for 7 to 8 minutes, until the meat is browned.
4. Add the wine. Raise the heat to medium-high and cook for 3 minutes, until the alcohol in the wine evaporates and the wine reduces by about ½.
5. Add the tomatoes, a pinch of salt, and some black pepper. Reduce the heat to low, cover the sauté pan, and cook for at least 1 hour, adding some water if necessary. Remove from the heat and set aside. Remove and discard the bay leaf.
6. In a medium (8- to 12-quart [7.6- to 11.4-L]) stockpot, bring the water and 1 tablespoon salt to a boil. Add the *Malloreddus* and cook for 3 to 5 minutes, until the pasta is almost al dente. (If you are using dry pasta, follow the package instructions.) Remove from the heat. Drain the pasta and add it to the pan with the meat sauce. Toss to combine.
7. Serve hot, sprinkled with the pecorino.

Malloreddus with Young Pecorino

Young pecorino is a semisoft sheep's milk cheese that has been aged for about a month and has a mild flavor and creamy texture. It is less tangy and milder in flavor than pecorino that has been aged longer. It also has more moisture (due to the fact that it is relatively young), and it melts easily. It is the perfect cheese for this pasta dish, which I call "Sardinian mac and cheese." The pecorino adds a lot of flavor to the pasta, and the creaminess makes the dish perfect for a comfort meal.

YIELD: 4 SERVINGS

- 1 gallon (3.80 L) water
- 1 tablespoon sea salt
- 3 cups (312 g) fresh *Malloreddus* (see recipe on p. 110) or other short pasta, such as shells or elbows
- 2 cups (200 g) freshly grated young pecorino
- Sea salt, to taste

1. In a medium (8- to 12-quart [7.6- to 11.4-L]) stockpot, bring the water and salt to a boil. Add the *Malloreddus* and cook for 3 to 5 minutes, until the pasta is almost al dente. (If you are using dry pasta, follow the package instructions.) Remove from the heat.
2. Drain the pasta, reserving about 1 cup (237 mL) of the cooking water.
3. Return the cooked pasta to the stockpot and add the pecorino. Add a little of the reserved cooking water. Stir well over very low heat, adding more of the reserved cooking water if necessary to create a thick cheese sauce. Add the salt to taste.
4. Transfer the pasta to a serving bowl. Serve hot.

Malloreddus alla Campidanese (with Sausage)

This is one of the most traditional dishes of the Campidano plain in Sardinia's south. The area has been Sardinia's granary since Roman times. This robust, yet delicate, sauce matches the weight of the pasta perfectly. The saffron perfumes the sauce, giving it character. Pair this dish with a medium-bodied *Carignano del Sulcis, such as Sardus Pater Is Solus.*

YIELD: 4 SERVINGS

- 1 tablespoon extra virgin olive oil
- 2 links mild Italian sausage, casings removed
- ½ medium onion, chopped
- 2 cloves garlic, minced
- ¼ teaspoon saffron (optional, but highly recommended), dissolved in 1 tablespoon water
- 1 (28-ounce [784-g]) can whole tomatoes, chopped
- 1 tablespoon sea salt, plus more, to taste
- Freshly ground black pepper, to taste
- 1 gallon (3.80 L) water
- 3 cups (312 g) fresh *Malloreddus* (see recipe on p. 110) or other short pasta, such as shells or elbows
- ½ cup (50 g) freshly grated pecorino, for sprinkling

1. In a large (6- to 7-quart [5.7- to 6.6-L]) sauté pan, warm the oil over medium heat. Add the sausage and cook for 7 to 8 minutes, breaking it up with a wooden spoon.
2. Add the onion and cook for 5 minutes, until it starts to soften.
3. Add the garlic and cook for 1 minute. Add the saffron, stir well, and cook for an additional minute.
4. Add the tomatoes with their juice and some salt. Stir well. Reduce the heat to medium-low and cook for 30 to 40 minutes, until the sauce thickens. Add the black pepper. Remove from the heat and set aside.
5. In a medium (8- to 12-quart [7.6- to 11.4-L]) stockpot, bring the water and 1 tablespoon salt to a boil. Add the *Malloreddus* and cook for 3 to 5 minutes, until the pasta is almost al dente. (If you are using dry pasta, follow the package instructions.) Remove from the heat.
6. Drain the pasta, reserving 1 cup (237 mL) of the cooking water.
7. Add the pasta to the pan with the tomato sauce. Toss, adding some of the reserved cooking water if necessary. Cook for 30 to 40 seconds, stirring.
8. Transfer the pasta and sauce to a serving bowl. Serve hot, sprinkled with the pecorino.

Pane Frattau

This typical Sardinian dish is like a light version of pizza. The egg adds protein and some richness. It is the perfect summer lunch: light, yet full of flavor. Pair with a rich Vermentino di Sardegna, such as Sardus Pater Lugore.

YIELD: 4 SERVINGS

FOR THE TOMATO SAUCE:

- 1 tablespoon extra virgin olive oil
- 1 clove garlic, minced
- 1 (28-ounce [784-g]) can whole tomatoes, chopped
- Sea salt, to taste

FOR THE *PANE FRATTAU*:

- 3 cups (711 mL) Vegetable Stock (see recipe in the Mini Meatballs recipe on page 66)
- 8 rounds *pane carasau**
- 4 large eggs
- 2 tablespoons extra virgin olive oil
- Sea salt, to taste
- ¼ cup (25 g) freshly grated pecorino, for sprinkling (optional)

TO MAKE THE TOMATO SAUCE:

1. In a medium (4- to 5-quart [3.8- to 4.7-L]) sauté pan, warm the oil and garlic over low heat until the garlic starts to sizzle.
2. Add the tomatoes and a pinch of salt. Stir well and cook for 20 to 25 minutes, until the sauce thickens. Adjust the seasoning to taste. Remove from the heat and set aside.

TO MAKE THE *PANE FRATTAU*:

3. Set 4 large plates next to the stove.
4. In a 12-inch (30-cm) pan, warm the Vegetable Stock.
5. Drop the rounds of *pane carasau* in the Vegetable Stock, 1 at a time, and cook each for about 1 minute, until softened.
6. Put a round of cooked *pane carasau* on each plate and spread 2 tablespoons of the Tomato Sauce on each round. Cover each sauced round with another round of *pane carasau*. Divide the remaining tomato sauce evenly among the plates.
7. Into a small bowl, carefully crack the eggs, taking care not to break the yolks.

8. In a medium (4- to 5-quart [3.8- to 4.7-L]) nonstick sauté pan, warm the oil over medium-high heat. Add the eggs. Add a pinch of salt to each egg and cook to the desired doneness.

9. Place 1 fried egg on top of the upper round of *pane carasau* on each plate. Serve hot, sprinkled with the pecorino, if desired.

*Pane carasau *is available at culinary stores, Italian groceries, and online from Gourmet Sardinia and Buon Gusto (see p. 260 for contact information).*

WILD FENNEL

Wild fennel is everywhere in Sardinia. Its playful fronds beckon drivers to pull over and gather some. And that is exactly what I do when I am in Sardinia. In the U.S., where wild fennel is difficult to find, I use the greens of regular fennel and simply chop them more finely.

Penne with Wild Fennel and Pancetta

This dish never fails to remind me of my friend Giorgio Congui, who first taught me how to gather wild herbs around his house in Crastu, in the interior of Sardinia. We would go herb gathering in the Sardinian sun and the fruits of our labors made the car smell like a perfumery. The best part—all those herbs would be used in that evening's dinner. The dishes were always simple, with no more than five ingredients or so, but supremely delicious.

In this dish, the richness of the pancetta is perfectly balanced by the freshness of the fennel. Pair this dish with Argiolas Costera, a lighter Cannonau di Sardegna, *for a quick and exquisitely satisfying meal.*

YIELD: 4 SERVINGS

- **2 tablespoons extra virgin olive oil**
- **2 ounces (57 g) pancetta, finely chopped**
- **1 clove garlic, thinly sliced**
- **½ cup (44 g) finely chopped whole wild fennel or the greens of regular fennel**
- **Crushed red pepper, to taste (optional)**
- **1 gallon (3.80 L) water**
- **1 tablespoon sea salt, plus more, to taste**
- **4 cups (11 ounces [312 g]) whole wheat penne or other short pasta**
- **½ cup (50 g) freshly grated pecorino, for sprinkling**

1. In a large (6- to 7-quart [5.7- to 6.6-L]) sauté pan, warm the oil over medium heat.
2. Add the pancetta and cook for 3 to 4 minutes, until the fat has rendered and the pancetta is starting to brown. Add the garlic and cook for 2 minutes, until the pancetta is brown and crunchy.
3. Add the fennel and crushed red pepper (if using), stir well, and cook for 3 minutes, until the fennel wilts.
4. In a medium (8- to 12-quart [7.6- to 11.4-L]) stockpot, bring the water and 1 tablespoon of salt to a boil. Add the pasta and cook until almost al dente, 1 minute less than the package instructions.
5. Drain the pasta, reserving 1 cup (237 mL) of the cooking water. Transfer the pasta to the sauté pan with the fennel and pancetta.
6. Toss the pasta and cook for 30 seconds, adding some of the reserved cooking water, if necessary. Adjust the seasoning to taste.
7. Transfer the pasta to a serving bowl. Serve hot, sprinkled with the pecorino.

Potato and Mint Ravioli

Potato and mint ravioli, called culurgiones, *are beloved in Barbagia, in Sardinia's interior, and Ogliastra, one of the least populated parts of Sardinia on the eastern side of the island.*

The mint gives the ravioli freshness and makes the flavor more interesting. In Sardinia, these ravioli are often served with a simple tomato sauce. I prefer them with a more robust sauce with more complex flavors, such as my Lamb Ragù (see recipe on p. 125).

YIELD: 4 SERVINGS (ABOUT 24 RAVIOLI)

FOR THE DOUGH:

- 1½ cups (210 g) *semola rimacinata**
- ¼ teaspoon sea salt
- 1 large egg
- 2 cups (474 mL) cold water

FOR THE FILLING:

- 1 pound (454 g) russet potatoes, peeled and cubed
- 1 teaspoon sea salt, plus more, to taste
- 1 large egg, lightly beaten
- 2 tablespoons freshly grated pecorino
- 2 teaspoons minced fresh mint
- Pinch nutmeg

TO MAKE THE DOUGH:

1. In a medium bowl, combine the *semola rimacinata*, salt, and egg. Add 1 cup (237 mL) of the water and stir. Continue adding water until the dough comes together and is not too firm to be kneaded. If the dough is too firm, add a little more water. If the dough is too soft and sticks to your hands, add a little more *semola rimacinata*. (The dough can also be made in a food processor or a stand mixer.)
2. Take the dough out of the bowl and knead it on a clean working surface for 10 minutes.
3. Wrap the dough in plastic wrap and refrigerate it for at least 20 minutes.

TO MAKE THE FILLING:

4. In a medium (8- to 12-quart [7.6- to 11.4-L]) stockpot, cover the potatoes with water. Add 1 teaspoon of salt. Bring to a boil and cook until the potatoes are done and a fork goes through them easily. Remove from the heat. Drain and let cool slightly.
5. In a medium bowl, mash the potatoes. Add the egg, pecorino, mint, nutmeg, and a pinch of salt. Stir to combine.

TO ASSEMBLE THE RAVIOLI:

6. Divide the dough into quarters. Roll out each quarter to 1/8-inch (3-mm) thickness and cut out circles using a ravioli cutter or small glass. You should be able to cut about 10 to 12 circles out of each piece of dough.

7. Place 1 heaping teaspoon of the filling on half of the circles.

8. Cover each filled circle of dough with another circle and press the edges together, closing the ravioli tightly. If the edges of the circles are too dry to adhere, wet them with a little water.

9. Place the ravioli on a floured baking sheet. The ravioli can be made several hours ahead of time and refrigerated. They can also be frozen for up to 4 weeks.

*Semola rimacinata *is finely ground semolina (durum wheat) flour. If you cannot find* semola rimacinata, *use ½ regular semolina flour and ½ all-purpose flour.*

Potato and Mint Ravioli in Tomato Sauce

This is a common pasta dish on Sardinian menus. The Potato and Mint Ravioli are tossed in a light tomato sauce for a simple, yet satisfying dish. Pair this dish with Argiolas Perdera, a light Sardinian red from the native monica grape.

YIELD: 4 SERVINGS

- **2 tablespoons extra virgin olive oil**
- **2 cloves garlic, thinly sliced**
- **1 (28-ounce [784-g]) can whole tomatoes, chopped**
- **1 tablespoon sea salt, plus more, to taste**
- **1 gallon (3.80 L) water**
- **24 pieces (1 recipe) Potato and Mint Ravioli (see recipe on p. 122)**
- **¼ cup (25 g) freshly grated pecorino, for sprinkling**

1. In a medium (4- to 5-quart [3.8- 4.7-L]) sauté pan, heat the oil and garlic over low heat.
2. When the garlic starts to sizzle, add the tomatoes and a pinch of salt and continue cooking over low heat for 20 to 30 minutes, until the sauce thickens. Adjust the seasoning to taste. Remove the sauce from the heat and set aside.
3. In a large (12- to 18-quart [11.4- to 17.0-L]) stockpot, bring the water and 1 tablespoon of salt to a boil. Add the ravioli and boil for 2 to 3 minutes, stirring to prevent the ravioli from sticking.
4. Drain the ravioli and transfer to the pan containing the sauce. Toss the ravioli with the sauce.
5. Transfer the ravioli and sauce to a serving bowl. Serve hot, sprinkled with the pecorino.

Potato and Mint Ravioli with Lamb Ragù

This is the perfect comfort dish for cool evenings. When paired with a robust Sardinian Cannonau, *such as* Nepente di Oliena, *the dish sings.*

YIELD: 6 SERVINGS

- 2 tablespoons extra virgin olive oil
- ½ small red onion, finely chopped (about ¾ cup [113 g])
- 1 clove garlic, minced
- 1 pound (454 g) lamb, ground or finely chopped
- 1 sundried tomato, finely chopped
- 1 (28-ounce [784-g]) can whole tomatoes, with juice
- Crushed red pepper, to taste (optional)
- 1 tablespoon sea salt, plus more, to taste
- Freshly ground black pepper, to taste
- 1 gallon (3.80 L) water
- 24 pieces (1 recipe) Potato and Mint Ravioli (see recipe on p. 122)
- ½ cup (50 g) freshly grated pecorino, for sprinkling

1. In a medium Dutch oven or heavy-bottomed pot, warm the oil over medium heat. Add the onion and cook for 7 to 8 minutes, until it softens and becomes translucent.

2. Add the garlic and continue cooking for 1 minute, until the garlic releases its flavor. Add the lamb and cook for 7 to 8 minutes, stirring, until the lamb is browned.

3. Add the sundried tomato, stir well, and cook for 2 minutes. Add the tomatoes and their juice, crushed red pepper (if using), and a pinch of salt. Cover and cook for at least 1½ hours, adding some water if the sauce becomes too thick. Add a grind of black pepper. Adjust the seasoning to taste.

4. In a large (12- to 18-quart [11.4- to 17.0-L]) stockpot, bring the water and 1 tablespoon of salt to a boil. Add the ravioli and boil for 2 to 3 minutes, stirring to prevent the ravioli from sticking.

5. Drain the ravioli and transfer to the Dutch oven containing the lamb ragù. Toss the ravioli with the ragù.

6. Transfer the ravioli and ragù to a serving bowl. Serve hot, sprinkled with the pecorino.

Ricotta and Greens Ravioli

These ravioli, which feature a delicious ricotta and greens filling, are quite common in Sardinia. While you can find ricotta ravioli in supermarkets, it is worth making them at home. Homemade ravioli always have more flavor and taste fresher.

YIELD: 4 SERVINGS (ABOUT 24 RAVIOLI)

FOR THE DOUGH:

- 1½ cups (210 g) *semola rimacinata**
- ¼ teaspoon sea salt
- 1 large egg
- 2 cups (474 mL) cold water

FOR THE FILLING:

- 2 quarts (1.90 L) water
- 1 teaspoon sea salt, plus more, to taste
- 1 bunch (about ½ pound [227 g]) beet greens, tough parts removed and green parts chopped
- ½ pound (227 g) fresh ricotta (preferably sheep's milk)
- 1 large egg yolk
- ¼ cup (25 g) freshly grated pecorino
- Pinch saffron

TO MAKE THE DOUGH:

1. In a medium bowl, combine the *semola rimacinata*, salt, and egg. Add ½ cup (119 mL) of the water and stir. Continue adding water until the dough comes together and is not too firm to be kneaded. If the dough is too firm, add a little more water. If the dough is too soft and sticks to your hands, add a little more *semola rimacinata*. (The dough can also be made in a food processor or a stand mixer.)
2. Take the dough out of the bowl and knead it on a clean working surface for 10 minutes.
3. Wrap the dough in plastic wrap and refrigerate it for at least 20 minutes.

TO MAKE THE FILLING:

4. In a medium (8- to 12-quart [7.6- to 11.4-L]) stockpot, bring the water and 1 teaspoon salt to a boil. Add the greens and cook for 4 to 5 minutes, until they are soft.
5. Drain the greens into a colander and set them aside to cool. Press the greens with a wooden spoon to squeeze all of the water out of them.
6. In a mixing bowl, combine the greens and all the remaining ingredients and stir well until the mixture is uniform.

TO ASSEMBLE THE RAVIOLI:

7. Cut the dough into quarters. Roll out each quarter to ⅛-inch (3-mm) thickness and cut circles using a ravioli cutter or small glass.

8. Place 1 heaping teaspoon of the filling on half of the circles.

9. Cover each circle of dough with filling with another circle and press the edges together, closing the ravioli tightly. If the edges of the circles are too dry to adhere, wet them with a little water.

10. Place the ravioli on a floured baking sheet. The ravioli can be made several hours ahead of time and refrigerated. They can also be frozen for up to 4 weeks.

*Semola rimacinata *is finely ground semolina (durum wheat) flour. If you cannot find* semola rimacinata, *use ½ regular semolina flour and ½ all-purpose flour.*

Ricotta and Greens Ravioli with Wild Fennel

This spring dish is sophisticated enough for a fine-dining restaurant, yet easy to prepare and perfect for home dinner parties. Chef Roberto Flore of the Sardinian restaurant Antica Dimora del Gruccione adds abbacasu, *a byproduct of making cheese, at the very end to bring the sauce together and add an element of tartness. Since* abbacasu *is not typically available in the U.S., I substitute Greek yogurt, which has a similarly tangy flavor.*

YIELD: 4 SERVINGS

- 3 tablespoons (45 mL) extra virgin olive oil
- 1½ cups (131 g) finely chopped wild fennel or the green parts of regular fennel
- ¼ cup (25 g) thinly sliced garlic scapes*
- ¼ cup (25 g) thinly sliced green parts of green onion
- 1 sundried tomato, finely chopped
- 1 tablespoon sea salt, plus more, to taste
- Freshly ground black pepper, to taste
- 3 tablespoons (45 mL) *Vernaccia di Oristano* or other dry white wine
- 2 tablespoons plain Greek yogurt
- 1 gallon (3.80 L) water
- 24 pieces (1 recipe) Ricotta and Greens Ravioli (see recipe on p. 126)
- ½ cup (60 g) Herbed Breadcrumbs (see recipe on p. 64), for sprinkling

1. In a large (6- to 7-quart [5.7- to 6.6-L]) sauté pan, warm the oil over medium-low heat. Add the wild fennel, garlic scapes, onion greens, and sundried tomato. Stir well.
2. Add a pinch of salt and a grind of black pepper. Cook 5 to 7 minutes, until the greens start to soften. Add the wine and cook for 2 minutes, until the alcohol has evaporated.
3. Remove the sauté pan from the heat. Add the yogurt and stir well until the sauce has a uniform consistency. Adjust the seasoning to taste. Set aside.
4. In a large (12- to 18-quart [11.4- to 17.0-L]) stockpot, bring the water and 1 tablespoon of salt to a boil. Add the ravioli and boil for 2 to 3 minutes, stirring to prevent the ravioli from sticking.

5. Drain the ravioli, reserving 1 cup (237 mL) of the cooking water. Transfer the ravioli to the sauté pan containing the sauce. Toss the ravioli with the sauce, adding some of the reserved cooking water as needed.

6. Transfer the ravioli and sauce to a serving bowl. Serve hot, sprinkled with the Herbed Breadcrumbs.

Garlic scapes are the twisty, curly green stems of the garlic plant. They are also sometimes called garlic shoots, stems, or spears.

Ravioli with Eggplant and Sausage

This rich and satisfying dish is perfect for winter nights. I first tasted it in the mountains of Sardinia on a cold winter night. The flavor was rich, but somehow the dish wasn't heavy. The secret is in the eggplant, which adds richness but also makes the dish lighter and more flavorful. Vegetarians can make the dish with eggplant only, leaving out the sausage.

Pair with a full-bodied red wine, such as Sardus Pater Kanai Carignano del Sulcis.

YIELD: 4 SERVINGS

- ¼ cup (59 mL) extra virgin olive oil
- 2 medium eggplants, chopped into small cubes (about 4 cups [328 g])
- 1 link mild Italian sausage, casing removed
- 1 clove garlic, thinly sliced
- 1½ cups (356 mL) dry white wine (such as *Vermentino*)
- 1 tablespoon sea salt, plus more, to taste
- Freshly ground black pepper, to taste
- 1 gallon (3.80 L) water
- 24 pieces (1 recipe) Ricotta and Greens Ravioli (see recipe on p. 126)
- ¾ cup (75 g) freshly grated pecorino, for sprinkling

1. In a large (6- to 7-quart [5.7- to 6.6-L]) sauté pan, warm the oil over medium heat.
2. Add the eggplant and cook for about 15 minutes, stirring occasionally so the eggplant cubes cook on all sides.
3. Add the sausage, breaking up the pieces, and continue cooking for 4 to 6 minutes, until the sausage is brown.
4. Add the garlic and cook for 1 minute. Add the wine and cook for 3 to 4 minutes, until the alcohol evaporates and the wine reduces by about ½. Add the black pepper. Adjust the seasoning to taste. Remove from the heat and set aside.
5. In a large (12- to 18-quart [11.4- to 17.0-L]) stockpot, bring the water and 1 tablespoon of salt to a boil. Add the ravioli and boil for 2 to 3 minutes, stirring to prevent the ravioli from sticking.
6. Drain the ravioli, reserving 1 cup (237 mL) of the cooking water. Transfer the ravioli to the pan containing the sauce and toss together, adding some of the reserved cooking water, as needed.
7. Transfer the ravioli and sauce to a serving bowl. Serve hot, sprinkled with the pecorino.

Rigatoni with Wild Boar Sauce

Wild boar is a winter delicacy in Sardinia, especially around Christmas. Many Sardinians still hunt and those who don't have friends who can give them a piece of wild boar for the holidays. This sauce, rich and robust, pairs well with full-bodied red wines, such as Carignano del Sulcis *or* Nepente di Oliena.

YIELD: 6 SERVINGS

- 1 pound (454 g) wild boar shoulder, cut into ¼-inch (6-mm) cubes
- 1 small onion, chopped
- 1 medium carrot, peeled and cut into ½-inch (13-mm) pieces
- 1 stalk celery, cut into ½-inch (13-mm) pieces
- 2 cloves garlic, chopped
- 1 teaspoon minced fresh rosemary
- 1 teaspoon minced fresh thyme
- ½ teaspoon chopped myrtle leaves*
- 3 cups (711 mL) full-bodied red wine (preferably the same wine you'll drink with the dish)
- 3 tablespoons (45 mL) extra virgin olive oil
- 1 small onion, chopped (about 1 cup [150 g])
- 1 (28-ounce [784-g]) can whole tomatoes, chopped
- 1 tablespoon plus 1 teaspoon sea salt, divided, plus more, to taste
- 1½ gallons (5.68 L) water
- 1 pound (454 g) rigatoni (about 6 cups)
- ½ cup (50 g) freshly grated pecorino, for sprinkling

1. Combine the wild boar, onion, carrot, celery, garlic, rosemary, thyme, myrtle, and wine in a glass bowl. Cover tightly with plastic wrap and refrigerate overnight.
2. Remove the wild boar from the marinade and pat it dry with a paper towel. Discard the vegetables and herbs from the marinade, but save the liquid.
3. In a large Dutch oven, warm the oil over medium-low heat. Add the onion and cook for 7 to 8 minutes, until it softens and becomes translucent.
4. Raise the heat to medium. Add the marinated wild boar and cook for 8 minutes, until it is browned well on all sides.
5. Add the reserved marinade. Raise the heat to medium-high and cook for 4 minutes, until the wine has reduced by about ⅓.

RECIPE CONTINUES ON PAGE 132

Rigatoni with Wild Boar Sauce *(CONTINUED FROM PAGE 131)*

6. Add the tomatoes and 1 teaspoon of salt. Bring to a boil. Reduce the heat to low, and cook for at least 1½ (and up to 3) hours. Adjust the seasoning to taste. Remove from the heat and set aside.

7. When the sauce is almost done, in a large (12- to 18-quart [11.4- to 17.0-L]) stockpot, bring the water and 1 tablespoon of salt to a boil. Add the pasta and cook to al dente, following the package instructions. Remove from the heat. Drain the pasta, reserving 1 cup (237 mL) of the cooking water.

8. Toss the pasta with the sauce, adding some of the reserved cooking water, if necessary.

9. Transfer the pasta and sauce to a serving bowl. Serve hot, sprinkled with the pecorino.

*Myrtle branches and leaves are available in many specialty stores.

Risotto with *Bottarga* (Mullet Roe)

It might come as a surprise to find risotto, which is generally considered to be a northern Italian dish, in a book about Sardinia. But Sardinia holds many surprises. One of them is that the area around Oristano and Cabras on the west coast grows quite a bit of rice. So, while not very common, rice and risotto do find a place on the Sardinian table. Of course, they are always combined with native ingredients—in this case, strong-flavored bottarga *(mullet roe), which gives the dish richness and makes it truly Sardinian.*

Pair this risotto with Karmis, a blend of vermentino and vernaccia. The wine is full bodied and has an almost savory character (from the vernaccia), so it pairs perfectly with the strong and salty bottarga.

YIELD: 4 SERVINGS

- 6 cups (1.42 L) chicken stock
- 3 tablespoons (45 mL) extra virgin olive oil
- ½ yellow onion, very finely chopped
- 1¾ cups (350 g) vialone nano or arborio rice
- 1 cup (237 mL) dry white wine
- Sea salt, to taste
- 1 tablespoon butter
- 2 teaspoons grated *bottarga,* for sprinkling

1. In a medium (8- to 12-quart [7.6- to 11.4-L]) stockpot, heat the stock over medium heat.
2. In a large (6- to 7-quart [5.7- to 6.6-L]) stainless steel sauté pan, warm the oil and onion. Cook over very low heat for 8 to 10 minutes, until the onion softens and becomes translucent.
3. Add the rice. Raise the heat to medium and toast the rice for 1 to 2 minutes, stirring so the rice does not stick to the bottom of the pan.
4. Add the wine. Raise the heat to medium-high and cook for 2 to 3 minutes, until the wine evaporates and you can no longer smell the alcohol.
5. Start adding the hot stock to the risotto, 1 ladle at a time. Continue stirring the risotto constantly after each addition. After each ladle of stock has been absorbed, add the next ladle. Add a pinch of salt.
6. After 14 to 15 minutes, the rice should be cooked. Test it by taking a bite to make sure that it is cooked, but not too mushy. Adjust the seasoning to taste. Remove the risotto from the heat, add the butter, and stir well.
7. Transfer the risotto to a serving bowl. Sprinkle with the *bottarga* and serve hot.

WILD ASPARAGUS

Wild asparagus is one of the delicacies of Sardinia that make a trip to the island well worth it. It grows spontaneously in the countryside in April, and you can see Sardinians of all ages combing the green grass for those tender spears. It takes a little while to learn how to find the asparagus, but once you do, you will be hooked. The reward of enjoying the asparagus right after you pick it will make you want to go out and find more!

Risotto with Wild Asparagus

This dish uses wild asparagus, which can be found at farmers' markets in the early spring. You can make the dish with regular asparagus, but keep in mind that the flavor will be more intense.

Pair the dish with a more robust Vermentino di Sardegna*, such as Sardus Pater Lugore. The green flavors of the wine match the flavor of asparagus perfectly.*

YIELD: 4 SERVINGS

- 1 quart (948 mL) water
- 1 teaspoon sea salt, plus more, to taste
- 1 pound (454 g) fresh wild asparagus, washed and tough stems removed
- 6 cups (1.42 L) chicken stock
- 3 tablespoons (45 mL) extra virgin olive oil
- ½ yellow onion, very finely chopped
- 1¾ cups (350 g) vialone nano or arborio rice
- 1 cup (237 mL) dry white wine
- 1 tablespoon butter
- ½ cup (50 g) freshly grated young pecorino, for sprinkling

1. In a small (3- to 4-quart [2.8- to 3.8-L]) stockpot, bring the water to a boil. Add 1 teaspoon salt and the asparagus and cook for 2 minutes. Remove from the heat. Drain the asparagus and shock the spears immediately by plunging them under cold running water.
2. Cut the cooked asparagus into bite-sized pieces and set aside.
3. In a medium (8- to 12-quart [7.6- to 11.4-L]) stockpot, heat the stock over medium heat.
4. In a large (6- to 7-quart [5.7- to 6.6-L]) stainless steel sauté pan, warm the oil and onion. Cook over very low heat for 8 to 10 minutes, until it softens and becomes translucent.
5. Add the rice. Raise the heat to medium and toast the rice for 1 to 2 minutes, stirring constantly so the rice does not stick to the bottom of the pan.
6. Add the wine. Raise the heat to medium-high and cook for 2 to 3 minutes, until the wine evaporates and you can no longer smell the alcohol.
7. Start adding the hot stock to the risotto, 1 ladle at a time. Continue stirring the risotto constantly after each addition. After each ladle of stock has been absorbed, add the next ladle. Add a pinch of salt.
8. After 14 to 15 minutes, the rice should be cooked. Test it by taking a bite to make sure that it is cooked, but not mushy. Adjust the seasoning to taste. Remove the risotto from the heat, add the butter and the cooked asparagus, and stir well.
9. Transfer the risotto to a serving bowl. Serve hot, sprinkled with the pecorino.

Seafood Pasta

This is the flagship dish of the restaurant Su Barchile, where Signora Maria Teresa and her son and daughter have been serving traditional foods with passion and conviction for decades. Su Barchile takes advantage of its proximity to the sea to serve up some excellent seafood dishes and showcase the bounty of this part of Sardinia.

This dish is served with macarrones de busa, *a thick, spaghetti-like pasta made by wrapping the dough around a bicycle spoke or knitting needle. The dough is made with semolina flour, egg, salt, and water. In the absence of* macarrones de busa, *you can use any thick pasta, such as strozzapreti and even bucatini. Pair this dish with a more robust* rosato, *such as Sardus Pater Horus, or a robust* Vermentino, *such as Sardus Pater Lugore.*

YIELD: 4 SERVINGS

- 3 tablespoons (45 mL) extra virgin olive oil
- 2 cloves garlic, thinly sliced
- 2 cups (480 g) canned tomatoes with juice
- 4 large shrimp, cleaned and deveined
- ½ pound (227 g) clams, washed
- 4 scampi, cleaned (feel free to substitute lobster or crayfish, as scampi can be difficult to find)
- Crushed red pepper, to taste
- 1 gallon (3.80 L) water
- 1 tablespoon sea salt, plus more, to taste
- 11 ounces (312 g) *macarrones de busa* or other thick pasta, such as strozzapreti

1. In a large (6- to 7-quart [5.7- to 6.6-L]) sauté pan, warm the oil and garlic over medium-low heat. Add the tomatoes and their juice and cook for 2 minutes, stirring occasionally.
2. Add the seafood and a pinch of crushed red pepper. Stir well, and cook for 4 to 5 minutes, until the clams open and the shrimp and scampi are cooked through. Discard any unopened clams. Remove from the heat and set aside.
3. In the meantime, in a medium (8- to 12-quart [7.6- to 11.4-L]) stockpot, bring the water and 1 tablespoon of salt to a boil. Add the pasta and cook until it is almost al dente, 1 minute less than the package instructions.
4. Drain the pasta, reserving 1 cup (237 mL) of the cooking water. Add the pasta to the pan containing the seafood. Toss together, adding a little of the reserved cooking water if necessary to create a sauce. Adjust the seasoning to taste.
5. Transfer to a serving bowl and serve hot.

Spaghetti with *Bottarga*

Bottarga is a true Sardinian delicacy. Bottarga di muggine *is the pressed and dried roe of gray mullet, which thrive on the west coast of Sardinia around the towns of Cabras and Oristano.* Bottarga *has a very strong flavor, so a little goes a long way. In this simple recipe,* bottarga *is the last ingredient to be added, as it should not be cooked. Make sure not to overcook the pasta. I prefer to use thick spaghetti, as it stands up better to the strong flavor of* bottarga.

Because of its strong flavor, bottarga *is a little difficult to pair with wine. But Sardinian* Vernaccia *is the perfect match: robust and flavorful, the wine can hold its own with the* bottarga. *The almost savory character of* Vernaccia di Oristano *complements perfectly the strongly salty character of the* bottarga. *I also love Karmis, the blend of vernaccia and vermentino produced by Contini. This wine is slightly less robust than* Vernaccia, *but it has some of the same savory aromas that complement* bottarga.

YIELD: 4 SERVINGS

- 1 tablespoon extra virgin olive oil
- 2 cloves garlic, minced
- ½ teaspoon crushed red pepper (optional)
- 1 gallon (3.80 L) water
- 1 tablespoon sea salt, plus more, to taste
- 11 ounces (312 g) spaghetti, preferably thick
- 2–3 teaspoons grated *bottarga*, for sprinkling

1. In a large (6- to 7-quart [5.7- to 6.6-L]) sauté pan, warm the oil and garlic over medium-low heat. Add the crushed red pepper (if using). Remove from the heat and set aside.
2. In a medium (8- to 12-quart [7.6- to 11.4-L]) stockpot, bring the water and 1 tablespoon of salt to a boil. Add the pasta and cook until it is almost al dente, 1 minute less than the package instructions.
3. Drain the pasta, reserving 1 cup (237 g) of the cooking water. Add the pasta to the pan containing the oil and garlic. Toss, adding some of the reserved cooking water if necessary.
4. Transfer the pasta to a serving bowl and serve hot, sprinkled with the *bottarga*. Adjust the seasoning to taste.

Spaghetti with Clams

In Sardinia, this dish is made with the tiny local clams known as arselle. *You can substitute any of the larger clams that are more commonly found outside the Mediterranean. The only requirement is that the clams be very fresh and open while cooking.*

The sprinkling of bottarga *adds richness to the dish and makes it more Sardinian, but the dish has a lot of flavor even without it. Pair this simple yet delicious seafood dish with Argiolas Is Argiolas or Contini Karmis.*

YIELD: 4 SERVINGS

- 2 tablespoons extra virgin olive oil
- 1 clove garlic, thinly sliced
- 2 pounds (908 g) clams, washed (about 20)
- ½ cup (119 mL) dry white wine
- 1 gallon (3.80 L) water
- 1 tablespoon sea salt, plus more, to taste
- 11 ounces (312 g) spaghetti
- 2 tablespoons fresh parsley, chopped
- 2 teaspoons grated *bottarga* (optional)

1. In a large (6- to 7-quart [5.7- to 6.6-L]) sauté pan, warm the oil and garlic over medium-low heat.
2. When the garlic starts to sizzle, add the clams and the wine. Cover the pan and cook on medium heat for 4 to 5 minutes, until the clams open. Discard any unopened clams. Remove from the heat and set aside.
3. In a medium (8- to 12-quart [7.6- to 11.4-L]) stockpot, bring the water and 1 tablespoon of salt to a boil. Add the pasta, stir well, and cook until it is almost al dente, 1 minute less than the package instructions.
4. Drain the pasta and add it to the pan containing the clams. Toss together. Adjust the seasoning to taste, taking care not to oversalt if you are adding *bottarga*.
5. Transfer the pasta to a serving bowl and serve hot, sprinkled with the parsley and the *bottarga*, if using.

Spaghetti with Crushed Red Pepper

This is a very simple yet satisfying dish. It can be found on almost any restaurant menu in Sardinia and it is also perfect for home cooks. It takes only minutes and because it uses pantry ingredients, it can be a quick and satisfying workday dinner. Pair with a fuller-bodied white wine, such as Sardus Pater Lugore.

YIELD: 4 SERVINGS

- ¼ cup (59 mL) extra virgin olive oil
- 2 cloves garlic, thinly sliced
- ½–1 teaspoon crushed red pepper
- 3 tablespoons (6 g) parsley, finely chopped
- 1 gallon (3.80 L) water
- 1 tablespoon sea salt, plus more, to taste
- 11 ounces (312 g) spaghetti
- ¼ cup (25 g) freshly grated pecorino, for sprinkling

1. In a large (6- to 7-quart [5.7- to 6.6-L]) sauté pan, warm the oil and garlic over medium-low heat. When the garlic starts to sizzle, add the crushed red pepper and parsley. Stir well and continue cooking for 2 to 3 minutes, until the flavors blend. Remove from the heat and set aside.
2. In a medium (8- to 12-quart [7.6- to 11.4-L]) stockpot, bring the water and 1 tablespoon of salt to a boil. Add the pasta, stir well, and cook until the pasta is almost al dente, 1 minute less than the package instructions.
3. Drain the pasta, reserving 1 cup (237 mL) of the cooking water. Add the pasta to the pan containing the oil, garlic, and parsley. Toss and add some of the reserved cooking water, if necessary. Adjust the seasoning to taste.
4. Transfer the pasta to a serving bowl and serve hot, sprinkled with the pecorino.

Spaghetti with Tuna and Olives

This is a dish typical of the town of Carloforte on the island of San Pietro. San Pietro is well known for its tuna. It is one of few places where fishermen still engage in the traditional ritual of mattanza, *the famous tuna hunt. Pair this dish with a robust Sardinian rosato, such as Sardus Pater Horus.*

YIELD: 4 SERVINGS

- 3 tablespoons (45 mL) extra virgin olive oil
- 2 cloves garlic, finely chopped
- 1 anchovy fillet (oil- or salt-packed)
- ½ cup (67 g) chopped green olives
- ¾ pound (341 g) fresh tuna, cut into ¼-inch (6-mm) cubes
- 1 gallon (3.80 L) water
- 1 tablespoon sea salt, plus more, to taste
- 11 ounces (312 g) spaghetti

1. In a large (6- to 7-quart [5.7- to 6.6-L]) sauté pan, warm the oil and garlic over medium-low heat. When the garlic starts to sizzle, add the anchovy and cook for 1 minute, until the anchovy dissolves.
2. Add the olives and tuna and stir well. Cook for 4 to 6 minutes, until the tuna is cooked on the outside but pink on the inside. Remove from the heat and set aside.
3. In a medium (8- to 12-quart [7.6- to 11.4-L]) stockpot, bring the water and 1 tablespoon of salt to a boil. Add the pasta, stir well, and cook until it is almost al dente, 1 minute less than the package instructions.
4. Drain the pasta, reserving 1 cup (237 mL) of the cooking water. Toss the pasta with the olives and tuna. Add some of the reserved cooking water, if necessary. Adjust the seasoning to taste.
5. Transfer the pasta to a serving bowl and serve hot.

Spaghetti with Wild Asparagus

This is the go-to dish of all Sardinians in spring, when wild asparagus grows everywhere in the countryside and everyone tries to get out and gather some. In this dish, I like to use a whole garlic clove, so I can remove it after it has given the oil some aroma. That way, the garlic does not interfere with the flavor of the asparagus, which is divine on its own.

Asparagus is notoriously difficult to pair with wine, but Sardinia has solved that problem. Vermentino di Sardegna, *a family of medium-bodied white wines, offers green aromas and flavors that perfectly complement the flavor of asparagus. This is a match made in Sardinia! Pair this dish with a* Vermentino di Sardegna, *such as Argiolas Costamolino or Contini Tyrsos.*

YIELD: 4 SERVINGS

- 3 tablespoons (45 mL) extra virgin olive oil
- 1 whole clove garlic
- 1 pound (454 g) wild asparagus, cleaned and cut into bite-size pieces
- 1 tablespoon sea salt, plus more, to taste
- 1 gallon (3.80 L) water
- 11 ounces (312 g) spaghetti
- ¼ cup (25 g) freshly grated pecorino, for sprinkling
- Crushed red pepper, for sprinkling (optional)

1. In a large (6- to 7-quart [5.7- to 6.6-L]) sauté pan, warm the oil and garlic over medium-low heat. When the garlic starts to sizzle, add the asparagus and a pinch of salt. Toss and cook for 3 to 4 minutes, until the asparagus starts to soften but is still crunchy. Remove and discard the garlic clove. Remove from the heat and set aside.

2. In the meantime, in a medium (8- to 12-quart [7.6- to 11.4-L]) stockpot, bring the water and 1 tablespoon of salt to a boil. Add the pasta, stir well, and cook until it is almost al dente, 1 minute less than the package instructions.

3. Drain the pasta, reserving 1 cup (237 mL) of the cooking water. Add the pasta to the asparagus. Toss and cook for 30 seconds, until the flavors blend. Add some of the reserved cooking water, if necessary. Adjust the seasoning to taste.

4. Transfer the pasta to a serving bowl and serve hot, sprinkled with the pecorino and crushed red pepper, if using.

Spaghetti with Zucchini and *Vernaccia di Oristano*

Vernaccia di Oristano is my favorite Sardinian wine to cook with. Its flavor is strong and robust and it elevates a dish, giving it more complexity. This simple dish benefits from the flavor of Vernaccia di Oristano and it is best paired either with the same wine used for cooking or Contini Karmis, a blend of vermentino and vernaccia.

YIELD: 4 SERVINGS

- 3 tablespoons (45 mL) extra virgin olive oil
- 1 medium onion, chopped
- 3 large zucchini, cut into quarters lengthwise and then sliced into ⅛-inch (3-mm) slices
- 1 tablespoon plus 1 teaspoon sea salt, divided, plus more, to taste
- 1 cup (237 mL) *Vernaccia di Oristano* or other dry white wine*
- 1 gallon (3.80 L) water
- 11 ounces (312 g) spaghetti
- 1 cup (100 g) freshly grated pecorino

1. In a large (6- to 7-quart [5.7- to 6.6-L]) sauté pan, warm the oil over medium-low heat. Add the onion and cook for 3 to 4 minutes, until it begins to soften. Add the zucchini and reduce the heat to low. Add 1 teaspoon of salt and cook for 10 minutes.

2. Add the wine. Raise the heat to medium-high and cook for 3 to 4 minutes, until the wine is reduced by about ⅓ and the alcohol has evaporated. Turn the heat down to very low and continue to cook for 5 minutes, until the flavors blend. Remove from the heat and set aside.

3. In the meantime, in a medium (8- to 12-quart [7.6- to 11.4-L]) stockpot, bring the water and 1 tablespoon of salt to a boil. Add the pasta, stir well, and cook until it is almost al dente, 1 minute less than the package instructions.

4. Drain the pasta and toss it with the zucchini. Cook for 30 seconds, until the flavors blend. Adjust the seasoning to taste. Remove from the heat. Add the pecorino and toss until the cheese melts.

5. Transfer the pasta to a serving bowl and serve hot.

*If you cannot find Vernaccia di Oristano, *use* Vermentino *or another white wine with fresh green flavors, but* Vernaccia *has a concentration that gives this dish richness.*

Tagliatelle with Walnuts

This traditional Sardinian dish bursts with earthy and satisfying flavors. It is a wonderful vegetarian option and a perfect quick lunch or dinner in cooler weather.

Pair with Cantina Pili Pujades Monica di Sardegna.

YIELD: 4 SERVINGS

- 3 tablespoons (45 mL) extra virgin olive oil
- 1 clove garlic, whole
- ½ cup (54 g) breadcrumbs
- 1 cup walnuts (about 3½ ounces [98 g]), lightly toasted and chopped
- 1 cup (237 mL) 2% or whole milk
- Freshly grated nutmeg, to taste
- Freshly ground black pepper, to taste
- 1 gallon (3.80 L) water
- 1 tablespoon sea salt, plus more, to taste
- 11 ounces (312 g) fresh tagliatelle*

1. In a large (6- to 7-quart [5.7- to 6.6-L]) sauté pan, warm the oil and garlic over medium-low heat. When the garlic starts to sizzle, remove it from the pan and discard. Add the breadcrumbs, stir well, and cook for 3 to 4 minutes, until the breadcrumbs become light brown.
2. Add the walnuts and stir well. Add the milk and nutmeg. Stir well and cook for 3 to 4 minutes, until the sauce thickens. Add the black pepper. Adjust the seasoning to taste. Remove from the heat and set aside.
3. In a medium (8- to 12-quart [7.6- to 11.4-L]) stockpot, bring the water and 1 tablespoon of salt to a boil. Add the pasta, stir well, and cook until it is almost al dente, following the package instructions.
4. Drain the pasta, reserving 1 cup (237 mL) of the cooking water. Toss the pasta with the breadcrumb and walnut mixture, stirring well until all the pasta is coated. Add some of the reserved cooking water, if necessary. Adjust the seasoning to taste.
5. Transfer the pasta to a serving bowl and serve hot.

*You can use dried pasta as well, but the dish has more character when prepared with fresh pasta. Fresh tagliatelle and other pasta are widely available in grocery stores.

SOUPS

Sardinian cooks get very inventive with soups. The term "soup" is Sardinia covers a wide variety of dishes—from flavorful, light soups to richer broths to baked dishes more akin to lasagne.

A unique hearty soup is *zuppa gallurese* or *zuppa quatta* (or *zuppa cuatta*), a baked dish of bread layered with pecorino that is cooked in vegetable or meat broth. *Zuppa gallurese* is usually served as a first course, but it's really a full meal, hearty and substantial.

Sardinian soups often feature the island's flavorful legumes, such as fava, garbanzo beans, and a variety of heirloom beans. Bean soups are often flavored with greens, including fennel, spinach, endive, or escarole. These nutrition-packed additions make these soups into a complete meal.

Soup lovers will find much to enjoy in the recipes that follow: new ingredients, new flavor combinations, and new textures. Those who are not soup lovers yet will be converted, because Sardinian soups are impossible to resist.

Artichoke Heart Soup

This light and flavorful soup is perfect any time of year. It takes virtually no time to prepare. It's a great start to any dinner or a terrific lunch served with some cheese and olives.

YIELD: 4 SERVINGS

- 3 tablespoons (45 mL) extra virgin olive oil
- 1 small onion, chopped (about ¾ cup [113 g])
- 2 cloves garlic, minced
- 12 ounces (341 g) frozen artichoke hearts, thawed and roughly chopped
- 5 whole canned tomatoes, chopped, with their juice (about 1 cup [240 g])
- 1 quart (948 mL) water
- 1 teaspoon sea salt, plus more, to taste
- 2 tablespoons *fregola**

1. In a medium (8- to 12-quart [7.6- to 11.4-L]) stockpot, warm the oil over medium-low heat. Add the onion and cook for 7 to 8 minutes, until it softens and becomes translucent.
2. Add the garlic and cook for 1 minute. Add the artichoke hearts and cook for 4 to 5 minutes, until they begin to brown.
3. Add the tomatoes and stir well. Add the water and 1 teaspoon of salt. Reduce the heat to low and cook for 20 minutes.
4. Add the *fregola* and continue cooking for 10 to 12 minutes, until it is cooked. Adjust the seasoning to taste.
5. Transfer the soup into bowls and serve hot.

**Fregola is available at culinary stores and online from Gourmet Sardinia (see p. 260 for contact information).*

Asparagus Soup

This delicious recipe belongs to Chef Roberto Flore of Antica Dimora del Gruccione. Roberto, who has deep knowledge of Sardinian culinary traditions, creates inventive dishes fit for his high-end restaurant. His dishes are interpretations of traditional Sardinian recipes and use local, seasonal ingredients. Roberto sources his ingredients very carefully, working with small producers in the area and often using heirloom ingredients that are on the verge of extinction. This great culinary artist is also a tireless advocate for traditional foods threatened by globalization.

Roberto adds small meatballs to his soup. The meatballs make it a full meal, but if you want a lighter lunch, leave them out. The soup is still delicious without them! Pair with a smooth Vermentino di Sardegna, such as Argiolas Is Argiolas.

YIELD: 4–6 SERVINGS

- 3 tablespoons (45 mL) extra virgin olive oil
- 1 medium onion, chopped
- 1 medium potato, peeled and cubed
- 2 cloves garlic, roughly chopped
- 10 mint leaves
- 1 pound (454 g) fresh asparagus, tough parts removed and the rest chopped, divided
- Freshly ground black pepper, to taste
- 1 cup (237 mL) *Vernaccia di Oristano* or other full-bodied dry white wine
- 5½ cups (1.30 L) water, divided
- 1–2 tablespoons high-quality extra virgin olive oil, for drizzling
- Sea salt, to taste
- 16–24 Mini Meatballs (see recipe on p. 66) (optional)

1. In a medium (8- to 12-quart [7.6- to 11.4-L]) stockpot, warm the oil over medium heat. Add the onion and potato and cook for 5 to 6 minutes, until the potato starts to soften. Add the garlic, stir well, and cook for 1 minute.
2. Add the mint leaves and most of the asparagus, reserving some of the tops for garnishing.
3. Add a grind of the black pepper and stir well. Cook for 2 to 3 minutes, until the asparagus starts to brown. Add the wine and cook for 2 to 3 minutes, until the alcohol in the wine evaporates.
4. Add 5 cups (1.19 L) of the water and bring to a boil. Reduce the heat to low, cover the stockpot, and cook for 12 to 14 minutes. Remove from the heat.

5. Let the soup cool slightly, and then transfer to a food processor or blender. Process the soup until smooth. As the processor runs, drizzle in 1 to 2 tablespoons of oil.

6. Return the soup to the stockpot. Add the remaining ½ cup (119 mL) water and cook on low heat for 10 to 12 minutes. Adjust the seasoning to taste.

7. Transfer the soup into bowls. Serve hot, garnished with the reserved asparagus tops and the Mini Meatballs, if using.

Bean Soup

Roberto Flore, advocate for indigenous Sardinian products, uses an heirloom strain of beans called pisu de cara *in this soup. You can use your favorite bean, but try to use beans that are not too robust in flavor (such as black beans). I prefer cannellini or borlotti, also known as cranberry beans.*

This and similar soups are traditionally cooked in a clay pot over a low fire (often in an open fireplace). I use a heavy Dutch oven, which keeps the heat constant.

YIELD: 4–6 SERVINGS

- 2 tablespoons extra virgin olive oil
- ½ small onion, chopped (about ⅓ cup [50 g])
- 1 clove garlic, sliced
- 1 tablespoon fresh parsley, chopped
- ½ cup (80 g) chopped cherry tomatoes
- Sea salt, to taste
- 2 cups (454 g) dry beans, soaked overnight in cold water
- 2 bay leaves

1. In a Dutch oven, warm the oil over medium-low heat. Add the onion, garlic, parsley, tomatoes, and a pinch of salt. Cook for 4 to 5 minutes, until the tomatoes release their liquid and the onion starts to soften.

2. Add the beans and bay leaves, stir well, and cook for 1 minute.

3. Add water to 1 inch (2.5 cm) above the beans and bring to a boil. Reduce the heat to low, cover the Dutch oven, and cook slowly for at least 2 hours, until the beans are cooked. Remove and discard the bay leaves. Adjust the seasoning to taste.

4. Transfer the soup to bowls and serve hot.

Bean and Cabbage Soup

This easy-to-make soup is a delicious lunch or dinner in cooler weather. The cabbage adds flavor to the beans and makes the soup more interesting.

YIELD: 4 SERVINGS

- 2 tablespoons extra virgin olive oil
- ½ large onion, chopped
- ⅓ cup (45 g) chopped prosciutto (about 2 slices)
- 2 cloves garlic, thinly sliced
- 1 head Napa cabbage, roughly chopped (about 5 cups [350 g])
- 1¾ cups (397 g) dry cannellini beans, soaked in cold water overnight
- 1 cup (240 g) canned tomatoes, chopped
- 3 quarts (2.84 L) water
- Sea salt, to taste
- Crushed red pepper, to taste (optional)

1. In a medium (8- to 12-quart [7.6- to 11.4-L]) stockpot, warm the oil over medium heat. Add the onion and prosciutto and cook for 5 to 6 minutes, until the onion softens and becomes translucent.

2. Add the garlic and cook for 1 minute. Add the cabbage, beans, tomatoes, water, and some salt. Bring to a boil and cook for at least 2 hours, or until the beans are fully cooked. Adjust the seasoning to taste. Add the crushed red pepper, if desired.

3. Divide the soup among 4 bowls and serve hot.

Beet Green and *Fregola* Soup (*Lampazu*)

This recipe is a very traditional one, made only in the small village of Isili in the interior of Sardinia. Bruno, my friend Sara's cousin, made it for me during a fantastic family lunch at the Olivario, which is Bruno and Sara's family farm house located in a rustic olive grove. Lampazu is a wild green that grows in the interior of Sardinia and was used in this soup as a result of lean times in the past. Lampazu cannot be found in the U.S., but substituting beet greens gives delicious results. Of course, if you want to try the real thing, head to Sardinia!

YIELD: 6 SERVINGS

- 2 tablespoons extra virgin olive oil
- 2 ounces (114 g) pancetta, finely chopped
- 1 medium red onion, chopped
- 1 pound (454 g) beet greens, tough middle stems removed and the green parts chopped
- Sea salt, to taste
- 2 cups (480 g) canned tomatoes in their juice, chopped
- 1 cup (190 g) large *fregola**
- 1 cup (246 g) fresh ricotta (preferably sheep's milk)
- Freshly ground black pepper, to taste

1. In a medium (8- to 12-quart [7.6- to 11.4-L]) stockpot, warm the oil over medium heat and add the pancetta. Cook for 5 to 7 minutes, until the pancetta is crispy.
2. Add the onion and cook for 5 minutes, until it starts to soften. Add the greens and a pinch of salt. Stir well and cook for 1 to 2 minutes.
3. Add the tomatoes and enough water to cover the greens. Bring to a boil over medium-high heat.
4. Add the *fregola*. Reduce the heat to medium-low and cook for 15 minutes, until the greens are wilted and soft and the *fregola* is fully cooked. Remove from the heat and stir in the ricotta. Add the black pepper. Adjust the seasoning to taste.
5. Transfer the soup to bowls and serve hot.

Fregola is available at culinary stores and online from Gourmet Sardinia (see p. 260 for contact information).

Fava and Pork Stew (*Favata*)

This recipe was given to me by Editta Costa, a passionate Sardinian cook who assured me that favata *is much better with cabbage (numerous versions of this recipe do not include cabbage). And Editta is right: The cabbage makes the dish lighter and more flavorful. Perfect for fall or winter days,* favata *pairs well with a well-structured* Cannonau, *such as* Nepente di Oliena.

YIELD: 6 SERVINGS

- 1 pound (454 g) pork steak, cut into 1-inch (2.5-cm) pieces
- 3 ounces (85 g) pancetta, finely chopped
- ¼ pound (114 g) mild pork sausage, casings removed
- 1 medium onion, chopped
- 2 tablespoons fresh parsley, chopped
- 1 pound (454 g) dry fava, soaked for 4 hours in cold water
- ½ teaspoon sea salt, plus more, to taste
- 2 fennel bulbs (including green parts) cut into halves lengthwise and thinly sliced
- ½ head cabbage, thinly sliced
- 10 mint leaves
- **Freshly ground black pepper, to taste**

1. In a large (6- to 7-quart [5.7- to 6.6-L]) sauté pan, combine the pork, pancetta, and sausage and brown on medium heat for 7 to 9 minutes.
2. Add the onion and parsley. Stir well to release any bits stuck to the bottom of the sauté pan and cook for 5 minutes, until the onion starts to soften.
3. Add the fava, ½ teaspoon of salt, and enough water to cover the beans and meat. Bring to a boil. Reduce the heat to low and cook for 10 minutes.
4. Add the fennel and cabbage and continue cooking for 20 minutes. Add the mint, stir well, and cook for 2 minutes. Add the black pepper. Adjust the seasoning to taste.
5. Transfer the stew to bowls and serve hot.

Fennel Soup

This is one of the many dishes that feature wild fennel, a common ingredient in Sardinian cooking. Calling this dish a soup is somewhat misleading, since it is quite thick and similar to lasagne. It is rich, yet fresh tasting—an intriguing and surprising combination. It is perfect for a summer day with a glass of Argiolas Perdera, a lighter red wine from the monica grape that shows best when slightly chilled.

YIELD: 4 SERVINGS

- 2 quarts (1.90 L) plus 2 cups (474 mL) water, divided
- ½ tablespoon sea salt, plus more, to taste
- ¼ pound (114 g) wild fennel or the greens of regular fennel, roughly chopped
- 8 tablespoons (119 mL) extra virgin olive oil, divided
- ½ small onion, chopped
- 1 clove garlic, thinly sliced
- 4 ½-inch (13-mm) slices of crusty white bread (about 10 ounces [284 g]), cut into cubes
- 6 ounces (170 g) young pecorino, freshly grated, divided
- Freshly ground black pepper, to taste

1. In a medium (8- to 12-quart [7.6- to 11.4-L]) stockpot, bring 2 quarts (1.90 L) of water and ½ tablespoon of the salt to a boil. Add the fennel and boil for 3 to 4 minutes. Remove from the heat. Drain, reserving 1 cup (237 mL) of the cooking water, and set aside.

2. In a small (2- to 3-quart [1.9- to 2.8-L]) sauté pan, warm 3 tablespoons (45 mL) of the oil over medium heat. Add the onion and cook for 4 to 5 minutes, until it starts to soften. Add the garlic and cook for 1 minute, until the garlic releases its aroma. Add the fennel and a little of the cooking water. Stir well and cook for 1 minute, until the flavors blend.

3. Preheat the oven to 250°F (120°C).

4. In a medium bowl, toss the bread cubes with the remaining olive oil. Place the cubes on a 9 × 11-inch (22.5 × 27.5-cm) baking sheet and bake for 30 minutes, until the bread is crunchy and starts to brown. Remove from the oven and set aside.

RECIPE CONTINUES ON PAGE 162

Fennel Soup *(CONTINUED FROM PAGE 161)*

5. Raise the oven temperature to 400°F (200°C). In a 9 × 9-inch (22.5 × 22.5-cm) baking dish, combine the bread, fennel and onion mixture, and half of the pecorino. Stir to combine.
6. Sprinkle the remaining pecorino on top. Add 2 cups (474 mL) of water to the baking dish and bake for 18 to 20 minutes, or until the pecorino is melted and golden brown. Remove from the oven. Add the black pepper. Adjust the seasoning to taste.
7. Transfer the soup to shallow bowls and serve hot.

Fregola in Cheese Broth (Fregola in Brodo)

In Sardinia, this dish is made with lamb or mutton broth. I have made it lighter by using a broth made from pecorino cheese. Pecorino broth is a great way to add flavor to any soup. I usually make this soup in cooler weather, as a start to a meal that includes a meat-based second course.

YIELD: 4 SERVINGS

- 2 quarts (1.90 L) water
- 8 ounces (227 g) pecorino rinds*
- Sea salt, to taste
- ¾ cup (143 g) large *fregola***

1. In a medium (8- to 12-quart [7.6- to 11.4-L]) stockpot, bring the water and pecorino rinds to a boil.
2. Reduce the heat to low and cook for 1½ hours, stirring occasionally so the cheese does not stick to the bottom of the stockpot.
3. Strain the broth into a clean medium (8- to 12-quart [7.6- to 11.4-L]) stockpot, discarding the rinds and any pieces of pecorino. Season with salt to taste.
4. Bring the broth to a boil. Add the *fregola* and cook until al dente, following the package instructions. Adjust the seasoning to taste.
5. Transfer the soup to bowls and serve hot.

*I save the rinds and hard pieces of pecorino, freeze them, and use them to make broth. If you do not have pecorino rinds, you can use pecorino, but make sure it's hard and aged.

**Fregola is available at culinary stores and online from Gourmet Sardinia (see p. 260 for contact information).

Garbanzo Bean Soup with Wild Fennel

This soup, traditionally served in the Montiferru region in west Sardinia, is a very satisfying winter dish, especially when prepared in the traditional way with lard or pork fat. Roberto Flore, the chef of Antica Dimora del Gruccione, made this soup for me on one cold April day, and it was the perfect soul food. The recipe is very simple and the flavors are surprisingly complex.

Garbanzos have a rich, earthy flavor that pairs well with a flavorful Cannonau di Sardegna, such as Argiolas Costera.

YIELD: 4 SERVINGS

- 1 tablespoon extra virgin olive oil
- 2 ounces (57 g) pancetta (or pork belly), finely chopped
- 2 cups (454 g) dry garbanzo beans (chickpeas), soaked overnight
- ½ teaspoon sea salt, plus more, to taste
- ½ cup (44 g) wild fennel or the greens of regular fennel, finely chopped

1. In a medium (8- to 12-quart [7.6- to 11.4-L]) stockpot, warm the oil over medium heat. Add the pancetta or pork belly and cook for 5 minutes, until the fat is rendered.
2. Add the beans and ½ teaspoon of salt. Stir well. Add water to about 1½ inches (3.8 cm) above the beans. Bring to a boil.
3. Reduce the heat to low and cook for 1 hour.
4. Add the fennel and continue cooking for 1 hour, until the beans are thoroughly cooked. Adjust the seasoning to taste.
5. Transfer the soup to bowls and serve hot.

Lentil Soup with Potatoes and Beets

This delicious soup tempts you from the moment you look at it. The beets and greens not only brighten it up, but also add flavor. The soup is a complete meal: It's full of protein, vitamins, and minerals, and nourishes both body and soul.

YIELD: 8 SERVINGS

- 1 tablespoon extra virgin olive oil
- 1½ ounces (42 g) pancetta, finely chopped
- ½ small red onion, chopped
- 2 tablespoons chopped fresh parsley
- 2 cups (320 g) cherry or grape tomatoes, chopped
- 2 cups (384 g) lentils, washed
- 2½ quarts (2.37 L) water
- 1 teaspoon sea salt, plus more, to taste
- 2 medium Yukon Gold potatoes, peeled and cut into ½-inch (13-mm) cubes (about 2 cups [300 g])
- 1 large beet, peeled and cut into ¼-inch (6-mm) cubes (about 2 cups [272 g])
- 2 large celery ribs, chopped (about 1 cup [240 g])
- ½ cup (95 g) large *fregola**
- 1 bunch beet greens, thick stalks removed and leaves cut into bite-sized pieces
- Freshly ground black pepper, to taste

1. In a medium (8- to 12-quart [7.6- to 11.4-L]) stockpot, warm the oil over medium heat. Add the pancetta and cook for 3 to 5 minutes, until the fat starts to render.
2. Add the onion and cook for 7 to 8 minutes, until it softens and becomes translucent. Add the parsley and tomatoes, stir well, and cook for 3 minutes, until the tomatoes release their liquid. Add the lentils, stir well, and cook for 1 minute.
3. Add the water and 1 teaspoon of salt and bring to a boil. Reduce the heat to medium and cook for 10 minutes.
4. Add the potatoes, beets, and celery and cook for 25 minutes.
5. Add the *fregola* and beet greens and cook for 10 minutes, until the *fregola* is cooked through. Add the black pepper. Adjust the seasoning to taste.
6. Transfer the soup to bowls and serve hot.

*Fregola is available at culinary stores and online from Gourmet Sardinia (see p. 260 for contact information).

Minestrone with Fava

This simple soup is a complete meal: The beans provide protein, and the beet greens add vitamins and minerals. You can substitute other greens (endive, kale, or spinach) for the beet greens, if you prefer, but you might have to adjust the cooking time.

Pair with a light-bodied Sardinian red, such as Argiolas Perdera.

YIELD: 4 SERVINGS

- 1 tablespoon extra virgin olive oil
- 1 thick slice pancetta, finely chopped (about ¼ cup [38 g])
- 1 small onion, chopped (about ¾ cup [113 g])
- 2 sundried tomatoes, finely chopped (about ¼ cup [14 g])
- 1 cup (150 g) dry fava, soaked for at least 4 hours (or overnight) and peeled, if necessary
- 1½ quarts (1.42 L) water
- 1½ teaspoons sea salt, plus more, to taste
- 1 bunch beet greens, thick stalks removed and the leaves cut into ⅛-inch (3-mm) strips (about 4 cups [152 g])
- ¾ cup (80–90 g) small pasta (such as ditalini or small shells)
- Freshly ground black pepper, to taste
- ¼ cup (8 g) chopped fresh parsley, for sprinkling

1. In a medium (8- to 12-quart [7.6- to 11.4-L]) stockpot, warm the oil over medium heat. Add the pancetta and cook for 3 to 5 minutes, until it starts to brown.
2. Add the onion and cook for 5 minutes, stirring occasionally. Add the sundried tomatoes, stir well, and cook for 2 minutes.
3. Add the fava, water, and 1½ teaspoons of the salt. Bring to a boil and cook for 20 minutes.
4. Add the greens and continue cooking for 10 minutes.
5. Add the pasta and cook until the pasta is al dente, following package instructions. Add the black pepper. Adjust the seasoning to taste.
6. Transfer the soup to bowls and serve hot, sprinkled with the parsley.

Minestrone with Garbanzo Beans

Another brilliant Sardinian creation, Minestrone with Garbanzo Beans, is more than a soup: It is a complete meal. The garbanzo beans add earthiness and richness and the vegetables and greens make the soup not only beautiful to look at but also healthful. Sardinian peasants knew how to eat well.

Pair with Argiolas Costera, a medium-bodied red that matches the richness of the dish.

YIELD: 6 SERVINGS

- 1 tablespoon extra virgin olive oil
- 1 thick slice pancetta, finely chopped (about ¼ cup [38 g])
- 1 small onion, chopped (about ¾ cup [113 g])
- 1 medium carrot, peeled, cut in half lengthwise, and then sliced
- 1 celery rib, sliced into ⅛-inch (3-mm) slices
- 2 sundried tomatoes, finely chopped (about ¼ cup [14 g])
- 1½ cups (341 g) dry garbanzo beans (chickpeas), soaked overnight
- 1½ quarts (1.42 L) water
- 1½ teaspoons sea salt, plus more, to taste
- ½ endive, washed and chopped into ½-inch (13-mm) pieces (about 6 cups [300 g])
- ¾ cup (80–90 g) small pasta (such as ditalini or small shells)
- Freshly ground black pepper, to taste

1. In a medium (8- to 12-quart [7.6- to 11.4-L]) stockpot, warm the oil over medium heat. Add the pancetta and cook for 3 to 5 minutes, until it starts to brown.
2. Add the onion, carrot, and celery and cook for 5 minutes, stirring occasionally. Add the sundried tomatoes, stir well, and cook for 2 minutes.
3. Add the beans, water, and 1½ teaspoons salt. Bring to a boil and cook for 1½ to 2 hours, until the beans are done.
4. Add the endive and the pasta and continue cooking for 10 minutes, until the pasta is al dente and the greens have wilted. Add the black pepper. Adjust the seasoning to taste.
5. Transfer the soup to bowls and serve hot.

Pea Soup with Pasta and Ricotta

Simplicity doesn't get any tastier than this. Even people who are not fans of peas find this flavorful combination irresistible. Try it! Pair with a flavorful Sardinian rosato such as Argiolas Serra Lori.

YIELD: 4 SERVINGS

- ¼ cup (59 mL) extra virgin olive oil
- 1 medium yellow onion, chopped (about 1 cup [150 g])
- 3 cups (435 g) fresh (or frozen and thawed) peas
- 1 (14-ounce [784-g]) can tomatoes and juice
- 1 quart (948 mL) water
- 1½ teaspoons sea salt, plus more, to taste
- 1½ cups (160 g) short pasta (such as medium shells)
- ½ cup (123 g) fresh ricotta (preferably sheep's milk), for sprinkling

1. In a medium (8- to 12-quart [7.6- to 11.4-L]) stockpot, warm the oil over medium-low heat and cook the onion for 7 to 8 minutes, until it softens and becomes translucent.
2. Add the peas. Raise the heat to medium-high and cook for 3 minutes.
3. Add the tomatoes and juice, water, and 1½ teaspoons of salt and bring to a boil.
4. Add the pasta and cook for 10 minutes. Adjust the seasoning to taste.
5. Transfer the soup to bowls and serve hot, sprinkled with the fresh ricotta.

Seafood Soup

Sardinia has as many variations of seafood soup as there are cooks. Each Sardinian adds something unique, finding a way to make the dish his or her own. But these additions are not simply flights of fancy. The choices are always guided by what is seasonally and locally available. Sardinian cooks have a finely tuned ability to use the ingredients available to them to their best, never wasting or exaggerating in anything. Feel free to use your favorite fish and shellfish in this soup. Play with your cooking, be a Sardinian!

For a delightful meal, pair with Sardus Pater Horus rosato.

YIELD: 4 SERVINGS

- 2–2½ pounds (0.91–1.14 kg) clams and mussels, washed
- ½ cup (119 mL) dry white wine
- 3 tablespoons (45 mL) extra virgin olive oil
- 2 cloves garlic, minced
- Crushed red pepper, to taste
- 2 cups (320 g) chopped tomatoes
- Sea salt and freshly ground black pepper, to taste
- 4 large slices crusty bread
- 2 tablespoons chopped fresh parsley, for garnish

1. In a large (6- to 7-quart [5.7- to 6.6-L]) sauté pan, combine the mussels, clams, and wine. Cover and cook over medium heat for 4 to 5 minutes, until the mussels and clams open. Remove the pan from the heat. Discard any mussels or clams that are not open. Drain, reserving the cooking liquid. Set aside.
2. In another large (6- to 7-quart [5.7- to 6.6-L]) sauté pan, warm the oil, garlic, and crushed red pepper over medium-low heat. When the garlic starts to sizzle, add the tomatoes.
3. Raise the heat to medium and cook for 7 to 8 minutes. Add the shellfish cooking liquid to the sauté pan and continue to cook for 2 minutes, until the flavors blend. Adjust the seasoning to taste. Remove from the heat.
4. In the meantime, toast the bread. (For additional garlic flavor, rub the toasted slices of bread with a whole garlic clove.) Place each slice of bread into a shallow bowl.
5. Distribute the clams and mussels evenly among the bowls. Divide the tomato sauce evenly among the bowls.
6. Serve hot, garnished with the parsley.

Zucchini Soup with *Fregola*

Inspired by Chef Roberto Flore's asparagus soup, I was tempted to see what would happen if I used zucchini instead. The first time I made this dish on a cold winter day in Chicago, it was so captivating that I decided to make it part of this recipe collection. The zucchini flavor comes through beautifully and the dish is light yet satisfying and comforting. This combination of soup and fregola *is the perfect beginning to a dinner with a meat second course.*

The green flavor of the soup makes it pair well with Vermentino di Sardegna*, a wine with herbal notes. Try it with Contini Tyrsos or Argiolas Costamolino.*

YIELD: 4 SERVINGS

- ¼ cup (59 mL) extra virgin olive oil
- 1½ medium yellow onions, chopped (about 2 cups [300 g])
- 6 medium zucchini, chopped
- 1 cup (237 mL) Vegetable Stock (see recipe in the Mini Meatballs recipe on page 66)
- 2½ quarts (2.37 L) water, divided
- Freshly ground black pepper, to taste
- 1½ teaspoons sea salt, plus more, to taste
- 1½ cups (300 g) small or medium *fregola**

1. In a large (6- to 7-quart [5.7- to 6.6-L]) sauté pan, warm the oil over medium heat. Add the onions and cook for 7 to 8 minutes, until they are is soft and translucent. Add the zucchini, stir well, and cook for 5 minutes, until they start to soften and release their liquid.
2. Add the Vegetable Stock and 1 quart (948 mL) water. Bring to a boil and cook for 10 minutes, until the zucchini are soft. Remove from the heat and let cool for 5 minutes.
3. Transfer the zucchini to a food processor and process until you have a thick and uniform purée. Add the black pepper. Adjust the seasoning to taste. Set aside.
4. In a medium (8- to 12-quart [7.6- to 11.4-L]) stockpot, bring the remaining 1½ quarts (1.42 L) water and 1½ teaspoons of the salt to a boil. Add the *fregola*, stir well, and cook until it is al dente, according to the package instructions. Remove from the heat. Drain, reserving 1 cup (237 mL) of the cooking water.
5. In a large (6- to 7-quart [5.7- to 6.6-L]) sauté pan, combine the zucchini purée and *fregola*. Warm the mixture over low heat, adding some of the reserved cooking water, if necessary. Cook for 2 minutes. Remove from the heat.
6. Transfer the soup to bowls and serve hot.

*Fregola *is available at culinary stores and online from Gourmet Sardinia (see p. 260 for contact information).*

Zuppa Gallurese (Zuppa Quatta)

This, THE most traditional dish of Gallura, was originally cooked by shepherds and farmers. And it tells the story of this part of Sardinia: When poverty was commonplace, nothing was wasted. Stale bread was combined with meat broth and pecorino cheese to make this delicious and satisfying dish. It's comfort food at its best!

Use bread with good texture, that's not too light and fluffy. Pair with a medium-bodied Cannonau di Sardegna, such as Argiolas Costera or Contini Tonaghe.

YIELD: 4 SERVINGS

- 3 tablespoons (6 g) chopped fresh parsley
- ½ cup (44 g) chopped fennel greens
- 2 sundried tomatoes, chopped
- 1 cup (100 g) freshly grated pecorino
- 8 ounces (227 g) *caciocavallo*, thinly sliced*
- Sea salt, to taste
- 2–3 tablespoons extra virgin olive oil, for brushing
- 1 pound (454 g) white bread, crust removed and sliced into ½-inch (13-mm) slices
- 1 quart (948 mL) homemade meat broth (preferably lamb)

1. Preheat the oven to 375°F (190°C).
2. In a medium bowl, combine the parsley, fennel greens, sundried tomatoes, pecorino, *caciocavallo*, and a pinch of salt. Set aside.
3. Brush the bottom and sides of a 9 × 9-inch (22.5 × 22.5-cm) baking dish with the oil. Layer ⅓ of the bread slices in the baking dish and sprinkle with ⅓ of the cheese and herb mixture. Continue layering, finishing with a layer of cheese.
4. Add the broth, making sure the bread is well soaked. Bake for 25 minutes, until the top is golden brown. Remove from the oven.
5. Serve hot in the baking dish.

*Caciocavallo *is a semiaged cow's milk cheese that melts very well.*

Secondi

AFTER YOU HAVE WITNESSED THE BOUNTIFUL *ANTIPASTI* and satisfying *primi,* it's difficult to imagine *secondi* (second courses) that can be equally exciting. But Sardinian cooks outdo themselves once again, creating tantalizing creations no food lover—no matter how full—can resist!

Following the traditional division of Sardinian cuisine into that of the land and that of the sea, the *secondi* in this section are organized into seafood and land-based dishes. Each is closely tied to a place and a way of life on the island . . . and tasting them will help you better understand Sardinia.

SEAFOOD

Seafood has long been one of the pillars of Sardinian cuisine. All along the island's pristine coast, seafood is at the center of every meal. The most common types of fish are sardines, mullet, tuna, Mediterranean sea bass, and sea bream. Because the fish in Sardinia is of such high quality and has a lot of flavor, it is often served simply with a drizzle of extra virgin olive oil and sea salt, preserving all of its natural flavors. One common preparation involves baking fish in a salt crust, with just enough parsley to brighten the flavor. When frying fish, Sardinian cooks prefer to use semolina (durum wheat) flour for a better crunch.

    A variety of other seafood delicacies are available along the coast. In the town of Alghero, the local specialty is lobster, prepared most often *alla catalana*, with olive oil, tomatoes, onions, and herbs. Around Cabras, on the west coast, mullet and mullet roe are found on nearly every table. Eels also feature prominently there. In Cagliari, the locals favor *burrida* and *ricci* (sea urchins). If you ever find yourself on the island of San Pietro, make every effort to get to Carloforte, as its tuna and tuna roe have no rivals.

    Wherever you go in Sardinia, seek out local flavors and do what the locals do: Put yourself in the hands of Sardinia's capable cooks and delight your taste buds.

Baccalà with Tomatoes, Olives, and Wild Fennel

Baccalà *(salted cod)* is prepared in many different ways around Italy. Each region, and even each area within a region, has its own recipe for the dish based on what ingredients are available locally. This recipe uses two common Sardinian ingredients: olives and wild fennel. If you cannot find wild fennel, substitute the greens of regular fennel.

This light and flavorful dish pairs well with a Sardinian rosato, such as Sardus Pater Horus.

YIELD: 4 SERVINGS

- 1½ pounds (681 g) salted cod
- 2 tablespoons extra virgin olive oil
- 1 medium yellow onion, chopped
- 1 (28-ounce [784 g]) can whole tomatoes, chopped
- 1 cup (134 g) black olives, pitted and coarsely chopped
- 2 tablespoons finely chopped wild fennel or the greens of regular fennel
- Sea salt and freshly ground black pepper, to taste

1. In a large, shallow dish, soak the cod in cold water in the refrigerator for at least 24 hours, changing the water twice. Drain and set aside.
2. In a large (6- to 7-quart [5.7- to 6.6-L]) sauté pan, warm the oil over medium-high heat. Add the onion and cook for 7 to 8 minutes, until it is soft and translucent. Add the tomatoes and cook for 5 minutes.
3. Add the olives and cod and cook for 15 minutes over medium-low heat. Add the fennel. Reduce the heat to low and continue cooking for 10 minutes. Remove from the heat. Add the black pepper. Adjust the seasoning to taste.
4. Transfer the dish to a serving platter and serve hot.

Calamari Stew

This dish, first made for me by Editta Costa, is easy and delicious. Everyone I have ever served it to adores it—even people who have never tasted squid and might never have asked for it otherwise. It is the perfect meal for a summer day since it can be served at room temperature. Try it and delight your taste buds.

To round out your perfect meal, pair with a delightful rosato such as Argiolas Serra Lori or Sardus Pater Horus.

YIELD: 4 SERVINGS

- 3 tablespoons (15 mL) extra virgin olive oil
- 3 sundried tomatoes, chopped
- 2 green onions, chopped
- Crushed red pepper, to taste
- 1 bay leaf
- 1 pound (454 g) squid, cleaned, washed, and cut into ½-inch (13-mm) pieces
- Sea salt, to taste
- 1½ cups (356 mL) water

1. In a large (6- to 7-quart [5.7- to 6.6-L]) sauté pan, warm the oil over medium heat. Add the sundried tomatoes and green onions and cook for 4 to 5 minutes, stirring occasionally.
2. Add a pinch of crushed red pepper and the bay leaf and cook for 1 minute. Add the squid and a pinch of salt and cook for 5 to 6 minutes, until the squid starts to brown.
3. Add the water, stir well, and cook on low heat for 20 minutes. Remove and discard the bay leaf. Adjust the seasoning to taste.
4. Transfer the stew to bowls and serve hot or at room temperature.

Fish in Salt Crust

Cooking doesn't get any simpler than this. Fish can be challenging for home cooks because it is so easy to overcook. But this dish is failsafe.

The salt crust keeps the fish moist and infuses it with flavor. Since the fish is the star of the show, pick your favorite fish and make sure it is fresh. I like sea bream, but Mediterranean sea bass also works. The important thing is for the fish to be relatively large (about 1½ pounds [681 g] or so), so the salt doesn't overwhelm it. Pair with Cantina di Mogoro Ajò, a flavorful white made from the native nuragus grape.

YIELD: 4 SERVINGS

- 2 pounds (908 g) coarse sea salt
- 2 (1–1½ pounds [454–681 g]) whole fish (sea bream, Mediterranean sea bass, etc.)
- 4 sprigs fresh parsley
- 4 sprigs fresh thyme or rosemary

1. Preheat the oven to 375°F (190°C).
2. In an ovenproof dish large enough to hold both fish side by side, spread a layer of salt about ¼ inch (6 mm) thick.
3. Place the herbs in the cavity of the fish. Place the fish in the dish, atop the salt, and pour the remaining salt over them, making sure to completely cover both fish. Make a salt crust by pressing the salt into the fish.
4. Bake for 40 minutes. Remove from the oven. Carefully break the salt crust and remove the herbs.
5. Transfer to a serving platter and serve hot.

Grilled Sardines

Sardines are a perfect addition to your diet. They are high in nutritional value and full of flavor. Simply grilled and served with a drizzle of lemon juice and some minced parsley, they can seduce any food lover. Serve them with a more robust white, such as Argiolas Is Argiolas or Sardus Pater Lugore, or a slightly chilled light Sardinian red such as Argiolas Perdera (from monica grapes).

YIELD: 4 SERVINGS

- Extra virgin olive oil, for brushing
- 1¼ pounds (568 g) fresh sardines
- 2 tablespoons chopped fresh parsley, for sprinkling
- Juice of 1 lemon, for drizzling

1. Brush the grates of a grill with the oil. Preheat the grill on medium heat.
2. Place the sardines on the hot grill and grill for 2 minutes on each side, turning them carefully so as not to break them.
3. Transfer the sardines to a serving platter. Serve them hot, sprinkled with the parsley and drizzled with the lemon juice.

Octopus, Potato, and Green Bean Salad

Octopus is one of those foods that food lovers adore when it is prepared well. This simple and easy-to-prepare salad can turn anyone into an octopus lover. Paired with Argiolas Is Argiolas, it makes a perfect cold lunch or dinner.

YIELD: 4 SERVINGS

- 1 pound (454 g) fresh octopus
- 5 teaspoons sea salt, divided, plus more, to taste
- ½ lemon, sliced
- 2 medium potatoes, peeled and cubed
- ¼ pound (114 g) fresh green beans
- 4–5 tablespoons (59–74 mL) extra virgin olive oil
- 3 tablespoons (45 mL) white wine vinegar

1. In a medium (8- to 12-quart [7.6- to 11.4-L]) stockpot, cover the octopus with water. Add 2 teaspoons of salt and 2 slices of lemon and boil for at least 1½ hours. When the octopus is tender, remove from the heat. Drain and set aside to cool slightly. Cut the octopus into bite-sized pieces.

2. In another medium (8- to 12-quart [7.6- to 11.4-L]) stockpot, cover the potatoes with water to about ½ inch (13 mm) above the potatoes. Add 2 teaspoons of salt and bring to a boil. Boil until the potatoes are cooked through and a fork goes easily through the pieces. Remove from the heat. Drain and set aside.

3. In a medium (2- to 3-quart [1.9- to 2.8-L]) saucepan, cover the green beans with water. Add the remaining 1 teaspoon of salt and boil for 3 to 4 minutes. Remove from the heat. Drain and set aside.

4. In a large bowl, combine the octopus, potatoes, green beans, oil, and vinegar and stir well. Adjust the seasoning to taste.

5. Refrigerate for at least 4 hours (or overnight). Serve chilled.

Mussels in Spicy Tomato Sauce

Mussels are best when prepared simply, so their flavor comes through. The crushed red pepper in this dish adds a nice kick to the sauce. With some toasted crusty bread, this becomes the perfect lunch. For a meal that will make you feel like you're lounging in a café on the Sardinian coast, pair with Argiolas Serra Lori rosato.

YIELD: 4–8 SERVINGS

- ¼ cup (59 mL) extra virgin olive oil
- 2 cloves garlic, thinly sliced
- 1 tablespoon tomato paste
- 1 (28-ounce [784-g]) can whole tomatoes, chopped
- 1 teaspoon sea salt, plus more, to taste
- Crushed red pepper, to taste
- 4 pounds (1.82 kg) mussels, cleaned and washed
- ½ cup (119 mL) water

1. In a large (6- to 7-quart [5.7- to 6.6-L]) sauté pan, warm the oil and garlic over medium-low heat. When the garlic start to sizzle, add the tomato paste, stir well, and cook for 1 minute.
2. Add the tomatoes and their juice and stir well. Add 1 teaspoon of salt and some crushed red pepper. Reduce the heat to low and cook for 20 to 25 minutes, until the sauce starts to thicken. Remove from the heat.
3. In another large (6- to 7-quart [5.7- to 6.6-L]) sauté pan, combine the mussels and water. Cover the pan and cook on medium-high heat for 3 to 4 minutes, until the mussels open. Remove from the heat. Discard any unopened mussels.
4. Add the tomato sauce to the sauté pan containing the mussels. Stir well and continue to cook for 4 to 5 minutes.
5. Transfer to a serving bowl and serve hot.

Sardines with Lemon, Garlic, and Parsley

Sardinia wasn't named for sardines, but sardines are a common fish on the island. They are rich in vitamins B12 and D and also Omega-3 fatty acids, so they are very healthful, especially when baked or grilled with no additional fat. Enjoy this dish with a tasty white wine, such as Contini Karmis or Tyrsos.

YIELD: 4 SERVINGS

1½ tablespoons extra virgin olive oil, for brushing
8 medium sardines, cleaned
2 cloves garlic, minced
½ cup (15 g) finely chopped fresh parsley
Juice of 1 lemon
2 tablespoons Homemade Breadcrumbs (see recipe on p. 65), for sprinkling

1. Preheat the oven to 375°F (190°C).
2. Brush the bottom and sides of a 9 × 12-inch (22.5 × 30-cm) baking dish with the oil. Arrange the sardines in a single layer and sprinkle with the garlic and parsley. Drizzle with the lemon juice and sprinkle with the breadcrumbs.
3. Bake for 20 minutes. Remove from the oven.
4. Transfer to a serving platter and serve warm.

Sea Bream with Red Onion

This recipe could not be any simpler. It is ready in half an hour and requires 3 ingredients. The flavor is unbelievable, considering the simplicity.

Pair this dish with the Vermentino di Sardegna *you're cooking with, such as Cantina di Mogoro Le Giare.*

◊◊

YIELD: 4 SERVINGS

- 2 (1-pound [454-g]) whole fish (preferably sea bream or sea bass)
- Sea salt, to taste
- Semolina flour, for dusting
- 4 tablespoons (59 mL) extra virgin olive oil, divided
- 1 large red onion, thinly sliced
- 1½ cups (356 mL) *Vermentino di Sardegna* or another dry white wine
- 2 sprigs fresh thyme

1. Preheat the oven to 375°F (190°C).
2. Wash the fish, patting them dry with paper towels. Sprinkle each fish's cavity with salt and lightly dust the outside with the semolina flour on both sides.
3. In a large (6- to 7-quart [5.7- to 6.6-L]) sauté pan, warm 3 tablespoons (45 mL) of the oil over medium heat. Add the onion and a pinch of salt and cook 7 to 8 minutes, until the onion is soft and translucent. Remove from the heat.
4. On the bottom of a 9 × 12-inch (22.5 × 30-cm) baking dish, distribute the onion evenly.
5. Return the sauté pan in which you cooked the onion to medium heat. Add the remaining 1 tablespoon of oil. When the oil is hot (but not smoking), add the fish and brown them well on both sides, about 2 minutes per side.
6. Place the fish on top of the cooked onion, pour the wine around the fish, and add the thyme. Cover the baking dish with foil.
7. Bake for 20 minutes. Remove from the oven.
8. Transfer to a serving platter and serve warm.

Striped Bass with Vegetables

This light and flavorful dish is common in the coastal areas of Sardinia. It pairs well with a flavorful white, such as Cantina di Mogoro Ajò.

YIELD: 4 SERVINGS

- 1 quart (948 mL) water
- 2 teaspoons sea salt, divided
- 1 small Yukon Gold potato, peeled and sliced paper-thin
- ½ small zucchini, sliced paper-thin
- 3 tablespoons (45 mL) extra virgin olive oil, for brushing
- 1½ pounds (681 g) striped bass fillets
- ½ cup (119 mL) dry white wine

1. In a small (3- to 4-quart [2.8- to 3.8-L]) stockpot, bring the water and 1 teaspoon of salt to a boil. Add the potato slices and cook for 2 minutes. Add the zucchini slices and cook for 1 minute. Remove from the heat. Drain the potato and zucchini slices and set aside.
2. Preheat the oven to 350°F (180°C).
3. Brush a 9 × 12-inch (22.5 × 30-cm) baking dish with the oil. Arrange the bass fillets (skin-side down, if they are skin-on fillets) in a single layer. Sprinkle with the remaining 1 teaspoon of salt.
4. Cover half the fillets with the potato slices and the other half with the zucchini slices. Pour the wine over the fish and vegetables and bake for 20 to 25 minutes. Raise the heat to broil and brown the tops of the fillets under the broiler for 2 minutes. Remove from the oven.
5. Transfer to a serving platter and serve hot.

Swordfish with Peas

In Sardinia, this dish is generally prepared with dogfish. Since dogfish is not easy to find in the U.S., I use swordfish. Both fish are members of the shark family, and their flesh is similar in texture and firmness. This dish pairs well with a full-bodied white wine, such as Sardus Pater Lugore, or a flavorful rosato, such as Sardus Pater Horus.

YIELD: 4 SERVINGS

FOR THE SAUCE

- 2 tablespoons extra virgin olive oil
- 2 cloves garlic, minced
- 1 (28-ounce [784-g]) can whole tomatoes, chopped
- 2 cups (290 g) fresh (or frozen and thawed) peas

FOR THE SWORDFISH

- 2 tablespoons extra virgin olive oil
- 1½ pounds (681 g) swordfish steaks
- Sea salt, to taste

TO MAKE THE SAUCE:

1. In a medium (4- to 5-quart [3.8- to 4.7-L]) sauté pan, heat the oil and garlic over low heat, until the garlic starts to sizzle. Add the tomatoes and their juice and continue cooking over low heat for 10 minutes, until the sauce starts to thicken.
2. Add the peas and continue cooking for 5 to 7 minutes, until the peas are cooked. Adjust the seasoning to taste. Remove from the heat.

TO MAKE THE SWORDFISH:

3. In another medium (4- to 5-quart [3.8- to 4.7-L]) sauté pan, warm the oil over medium heat. Add the swordfish and cook until browned on both sides, 3 to 4 minutes per side. Remove from the heat.
4. Add the swordfish to the sauté pan containing the tomato sauce, making sure the fish is covered in sauce. Cook on low heat for 7 to 8 minutes, until the fish is cooked through.
5. Transfer the fish and sauce to a deep serving platter and serve hot.

POULTRY

Traditional Sardinian cooking doesn't use much poultry. Many recipes use rabbit, however, which is difficult to find in North America. For this cookbook, I have taken several popular rabbit recipes and modified them to be prepared with chicken. The flavor of these dishes is milder when prepared with chicken. If you prefer, you can substitute rabbit for chicken in any of these recipes.

Braised Chicken with Myrtle and Red Wine

This dish contains some common Sardinian ingredients: myrtle, sundried tomatoes, and red wine. It is easy to make and absolutely delicious. Pair with Argiolas Perdera, a light and flavorful red from the native monica grape.

YIELD: 4–6 SERVINGS

- 2 tablespoons extra virgin olive oil
- 1 whole chicken, cut up
- 3 cloves garlic, sliced
- 1 branch dried myrtle*
- 2 cups (474 mL) dry red wine (preferably Monica di Sardegna)
- 2 sundried tomatoes, chopped
- 1 tablespoon chopped fresh parsley
- Sea salt, to taste
- Freshly ground black pepper, to taste

1. Preheat the oven to 375°F (190°C).
2. In a large (6- to 7-quart [5.7- to 6.6-L]) ovensafe sauté pan, warm the oil over medium heat. Add the chicken pieces and cook for 7 to 8 minutes, turning halfway through, until they are browned on all sides.
3. Add the garlic and myrtle, stirring well to remove any browned bits from the bottom of the pan, and cook for 2 minutes. Add the red wine and cook for 2 to 3 minutes, until the alcohol has evaporated.
4. Add the sundried tomatoes, parsley, and a pinch of salt. Stir well, cover the sauté pan, and bake for 45 minutes.
5. Remove the sauté pan from the oven. Remove the chicken from the sauté pan. Place it on a deep serving platter and cover it with foil. Set aside.
6. Cook the red wine sauce over medium heat for 4 to 5 minutes, until it reduces by about 1/3. Remove the pan from the heat. Add the black pepper. Adjust the seasoning to taste. Transfer the sauce to a small pitcher.
7. Serve hot, with the sauce drizzled over the chicken.

*Myrtle branches and leaves are available in many specialty stores.

Chicken with Capers

You only need one word to describe this dish: deliziosissimo! *It always surprises me how a simple combination of a few ingredients can offer such deep, satisfying flavor. But don't just listen to me—try it for yourself. Pair with a Monica di Sardegna, such as Argiolas Perdera.*

YIELD: 4 SERVINGS

- 3 tablespoons (45 mL) extra virgin olive oil
- 1 whole chicken, cut up
- 1 medium yellow onion, chopped
- 2 tablespoons salt-packed capers, rinsed and chopped
- 2 cloves garlic, minced
- 2 bay leaves
- 1 teaspoon sea salt, plus more, to taste
- 2 tablespoons red wine vinegar
- 1 cup (237 mL) water
- Freshly ground black pepper, to taste

1. In a Dutch oven, warm the oil over medium heat. Add the chicken pieces and brown well on all sides, 3 to 4 minutes per side.
2. Add the onion and capers, stir well, and cook for 3 minutes, until the onion starts to soften. Add the garlic and cook for 1 minute.
3. Add the bay leaves and 1 teaspoon salt, stir well, and cook for 1 minute.
4. Add the vinegar and water. Reduce the heat to low, cover, and cook for 25 minutes.
5. Uncover the Dutch oven and cook for 5 minutes, until the liquid has reduced by about ⅓. Remove and discard the bay leaves. Add the black pepper. Adjust the seasoning to taste.
6. Transfer to a deep serving platter and serve hot.

Chicken with Tomatoes and Olives

This is another delicious and easy recipe that uses ingredients common in Sardinian cooking: sundried tomatoes, red wine, and olives. The tomatoes and olives give the dish richness and complexity.

Pair with Cantina Pili Pujades Monica di Sardegna, a medium-bodied flavorful red.

YIELD: 6 SERVINGS

- 2 tablespoons extra virgin olive oil
- ½ medium onion, chopped
- 1 sundried tomato, chopped
- 2 tablespoons chopped fresh parsley
- 1 clove garlic, minced
- 1 whole chicken, cut up
- 1 cup (237 mL) dry red wine
- 1 bay leaf
- ½ teaspoon minced fresh thyme
- ½ teaspoon minced fresh rosemary
- 4 ripe tomatoes, chopped*
- 1 tablespoon red wine vinegar
- ½ teaspoon sea salt, plus more, to taste
- ½ cup (119 mL) water (optional)
- ½ cup (67 g) chopped black or green olives

1. In a large (6- to 7-quart [5.7- to 6.6-L]) sauté pan, warm the oil over medium-low heat. Add the onion and cook for 4 to 5 minutes, until it starts to soften. Add the sundried tomato, parsley, and garlic, and cook for 2 minutes, stirring constantly.
2. Add the chicken and cook for 4 to 5 minutes, until it is browned. Turn the chicken pieces over and cook for 4 to 5 minutes, until they are well browned on both sides.
3. Add the wine. Stir well to release any browned bits from the bottom of the pan and cook for 2 to 3 minutes, until the wine reduces by ⅓.
4. Add the bay leaf, thyme, and rosemary, and stir. Reduce the heat to low, cover the sauté pan, and cook for 10 minutes.
5. Add the tomatoes, vinegar, and ½ teaspoon of salt. Stir well, cover the sauté pan, and cook for 10 minutes, adding the water if necessary.
6. Add the olives and cook, uncovered, for 5 minutes, until the sauce thickens. Remove and discard the bay leaf. Adjust the seasoning to taste.
7. Transfer the chicken and sauce to a deep serving platter and serve hot.

*If tomatoes are not in season, use high-quality Italian canned tomatoes.

Chicken with *Vernaccia di Oristano*

Vernaccia di Oristano is one of my favorite wines to cook with. It is a robust wine with a lot of flavor. It has a slightly savory and briny taste, so it adds that flavor to meats like chicken which do not have a strong flavor of their own.

Pair with Contini Karmis, a flavorful blend of vernaccia and vermentino.

YIELD: 4 SERVINGS

- 2 tablespoons extra virgin olive oil
- 1 medium yellow onion, chopped
- 1 whole chicken, cut up
- 2 cups (474 mL) *Vernaccia di Oristano*
- 1 teaspoon sea salt, plus more, to taste

1. In a large (6- to 7-quart [5.7- to 6.6-L]) sauté pan, warm the oil over medium heat. Add the onion and cook for 3 to 4 minutes, until it starts to soften.
2. Add the chicken and cook until well browned on all sides, about 7 to 8 minutes.
3. Add the wine. Scrape any chicken pieces from the bottom of the sauté pan, and cook for 3 minutes, until the wine is reduced by about ⅓.
4. Add 1 teaspoon of salt. Cover the pan, reduce the heat to low, and cook for 30 minutes, until the chicken is completely done. Remove from the heat. Adjust the seasoning to taste.
5. Transfer to a deep serving platter and serve hot.

MEATS

Traditional Sardinian cooking was closely tied to the lives of the island's shepherds and farmers, most of whom lived in the interior. Thus, it should come as no surprise that meat makes a frequent appearance in traditional dishes. Many of the most traditional Sardinian dishes are simple preparations of meat, spit-roasting being the most common.

The most famous dish of the island is *porcheddu*, a spit-roasted suckling pig. The dish, which in the past was only served on special occasions, can now be found on many restaurant menus. But the best *porcheddu* is found in the interior of the island, at *agriturismi* (rural family-owned farm holidays) that cook locally raised suckling pigs over a slow fire for hours and hours. The skin becomes crispy and crackles with every bite, and the meat is tender and flavorful, without too much fat. Traditionalists still insist that the roast be infused with myrtle.

Lamb and goat are also common, especially for celebrations and special occasions. Both are made in a variety of ways, either simply roasted with olives or herbs or slowly simmered in wine and flavorful sauces.

Cinghiale (wild boar) is another specialty, cooked either in wine or included in meat sauces, especially during the fall and winter hunting season. But don't expect to find wild boar in butcher shops in Sardinia. It takes a special license for butchers to sell it, so most Sardinians get it from friends and family who hunt. That's just more proof of how closely Sardinia's food and culture are connected.

SANGUINACCIO (BLOOD SAUSAGE)

Sanguinaccio, or blood sausage, is a prized Sardinian delicacy—especially in the interior of the island, which has a rich shepherd culture. In the past, when lambs were slaughtered, their blood was boiled with wild mint and onion until it reached a soft omelete-like consistency and was served on thick slices of bread. It used to be made at home, just like any other food. Nowadays, because of sanitation laws, it is produced by certified producers, but it remains an artisanal product.

In the Santu Lussurgiu area, where I first tasted *sanguinaccio*, the sausage is sweetened by adding chocolate and raisins. Even though it is sweet, it is served as an *antipasto*. Roberto Flore, the chef of Antica Dimora del Gruccione, serves small pieces of sweet *sanguinaccio* on cabbage leaves. The bitter and sour flavors of the cabbage complement the richness and sweetness of the sausage and lighten the dish.

At first, *sanguinaccio* might not sound appealing. Calling it "blood sausage" certainly doesn't help. But it's worth a try. The flavor is rich and complex, and eating it is a memorable experience.

Goat with Wild Fennel

Goat and kid are common meats in Sardinia, especially in the interior, where the cooking tends to be more meat based. Most of the preparations are simple and highlight the quality of the meat. This recipe can also be prepared with spring lamb, but it is more traditionally prepared with goat. It was inspired by a goat and fennel dish that I first tasted at Su Gologone and that has stayed with me ever since.

Pair with a robust Sardinian red, such as Sardus Pater Arruga or Argiolas Korem.

YIELD: 4 SERVINGS

- 1 quart (948 mL) water
- 2 cups (174 g) chopped wild fennel or the greens of regular fennel
- 2 tablespoons extra virgin olive oil
- 1 small red onion, chopped
- 2 cloves garlic, thinly sliced
- 1 pound (454 g) goat, cut into ½-inch (13-mm) pieces
- 1 cup (237 g) dry white wine
- 1 teaspoon sea salt, plus more, to taste

1. In a medium (8- to 12-quart [7.6- to 11.4-L]) stockpot, boil the water. Add the fennel and cook for 2 minutes. Remove from the heat. Drain, reserving the cooking water. Set the fennel aside.
2. In a Dutch oven, warm the oil over medium heat. Add the onion and cook for 4 to 5 minutes, until it starts to soften. Add the garlic and cook for 1 minute.
3. Add the goat and brown well on all sides, about 8 to 10 minutes.
4. Add the wine and cook for 3 minutes, until the alcohol in the wine evaporates and the wine reduces by about ⅓.
5. Add 1 teaspoon of salt and stir well. Reduce the heat to low, cover the Dutch oven, and cook for at least 1½ hours, occasionally adding some of the fennel cooking water.
6. When the meat is almost done, add the fennel and cook, uncovered, for 10 minutes. Remove from the heat. Adjust the seasoning to taste.
7. Transfer to a serving bowl and serve hot.

CORDULA

Sardinian cooking makes abundant use of internal organs. After all, poverty plagued much of the island for a long time, and no part of a slaughtered animal was wasted. *Cordula*, a braid of young lamb intestines, is a Sardinian delicacy, usually served on holidays such as Christmas and Easter. *Cordula* can be prepared with peas or simply roasted.

For *cordula* with peas, the *cordula* is first boiled in water and vinegar for 5 to 6 minutes. It is then browned in oil and flavored with onion, garlic, rosemary, and Sardinian sundried tomatoes. Some cooks add a full-bodied, dry white wine, such as *Vernaccia di Oristano*, to the pan for additional flavor. After the *cordula* has cooked for several minutes, add the fresh peas. Reduce the heat to low, cover the pot, and cook for another 10 minutes or so, until the peas are done.

The other way to cook *cordula* is to simply roast it with garlic, rosemary, sage, abundant salt, freshly ground black pepper, and a drizzle of extra virgin olive oil. This makes it perfectly crunchy on the outside and gives it a more concentrated flavor. Roasted *cordula* pairs really well with a robust Sardinian red wine, such as Sardus Pater Arruga. The richness of the *cordula* complements the significant tannins in the wine.

Sometimes, other lamb organs (the heart, lung, and kidneys) are skewered and wrapped in the animal's intestines. This variation is usually roasted. It also pairs well with a full-bodied Sardinian red, such as Sardus Pater Arruga or Capichera Mantènghja.

Lamb Stew

*Boiled lamb (*pecora bollita*), as this dish is called in Sardinia, sounds a bit uninspiring. But nothing could be further from the truth. This dish is rich is flavor and the perfect* secondo *after a light pasta. Calling it a stew does not do it justice. It is really meat cooked in liquid and served with some of the cooking liquid. It is tender and succulent.*

Traditionally, the vegetables the meat was cooked with were also served in the dish. But, as Chef Roberto Flore of Antica Dimora del Gruccione points out, it's a little visually unappealing to serve vegetables that have been boiled for 3 hours. They have lost all of their color and are falling apart. So, I discard the cooking vegetables and add fresh ones to preserve their color and integrity. This gives the dish great visual appeal.

Pair with a full-bodied red, such as Sardus Pater Arruga, for a true Sardinian meal.

YIELD: 4 SERVINGS

- 1 celery rib, cut in half
- 1 carrot, cut in half
- 1 small onion
- ½ head garlic
- 2 sundried tomatoes
- ½ cup (44 g) fennel greens, finely chopped
- 6 small potatoes, peeled and halved, divided
- 2½ pounds (1.14 kg) bone-in lamb (ribs, shoulder chops)
- 2 teaspoons sea salt, plus more, to taste

1. In a medium (8- to 12-quart [7.6- to 11.4-L]) stockpot, combine the celery, carrot, onion, garlic, sundried tomatoes, fennel, and 2 of the potatoes. Add water to about 1½ inches (3.8 cm) above the vegetables and bring to a boil.
2. Add the lamb and 2 teaspoons of salt. Reduce the heat to low and cook for 2 to 2½ hours, skimming off the fat and impurities that rise to the surface. Remove and discard the vegetables and aromatics.
3. Add the remaining 4 potatoes and cook for 20 minutes, until the potatoes are done. Remove from the heat. Drain, reserving the cooking liquid.
4. Transfer to a serving bowl, adding back some of the cooking liquid. Adjust the seasoning to taste. Serve hot.

Lamb with Fennel and Sundried Tomatoes

This delicious dish includes some of Sardinia's most common ingredients: fennel and sundried tomatoes. Both make the dish very Mediterranean. Pair with Sardus Pater Is Solus or Capichera Assajè.

YIELD: 4 SERVINGS

- 1 quart (948 mL) water
- 1 teaspoon sea salt, plus more, to taste
- 1 fennel bulb, quartered and sliced into ¼-inch (6-mm) slices
- 2 tablespoons extra virgin olive oil
- 1 small onion, chopped
- 1½ pounds (681 g) lamb stew meat, cut into ½-inch (13-mm) pieces
- 3 sundried tomatoes, chopped
- 1 cup (237 mL) dry white wine

1. In a medium (8- to 12-quart [7.6- to 11.4-L]) stockpot, bring the water and 1 teaspoon of salt to a boil. Add the fennel and boil for 2 to 3 minutes. Remove from the heat. Drain, reserving the cooking water. Set the fennel aside.
2. In a medium Dutch oven, warm the oil over medium heat. Add the onion and cook for 4 to 5 minutes, until it starts to soften.
3. Add the lamb and cook for 7 to 8 minutes, until the lamb is well browned. Add the sundried tomatoes, stir well, and cook for 2 minutes.
4. Add the wine and cook for 3 to 4 minutes, until the alcohol in the wine evaporates and the wine is reduced by about ⅓.
5. Add 1½ cups (356 mL) of the cooking water and a pinch of salt. Reduce the heat to low, cover, and cook for about 1½ hours, adding more of the cooking water, if necessary.
6. Add the fennel. Stir well and continue cooking, uncovered, for 10 minutes. Adjust the seasoning to taste.
7. Transfer the lamb to a serving bowl and serve hot.

Lamb Stew with Potatoes

Lamb is one of the delicacies of Sardinia, and no holiday feast is complete without it. "Spring" lamb is available in Sardinia during the Christmas and Easter seasons. It cooks much faster than regular lamb and has a more delicate flavor.

This dish pairs well with a well-structured red wine, such as Cannonau di Sardegna. *Try it with* Nepente di Oliena, *a wine that is the essence of Sardinia.*

YIELD: 4 SERVINGS

- 2 tablespoons extra virgin olive oil
- 1 medium onion, chopped
- 1 pound (454 g) spring lamb, cut into 1-inch (2.5-cm) cubes
- 1 cup (237 mL) dry white wine
- 4 medium Yukon Gold potatoes, peeled and cut into ½-inch (13-mm) cubes
- 1 tablespoon tomato paste, diluted in 2 cups (474 mL) warm water
- 1 teaspoon sea salt, plus more, to taste

1. In a medium Dutch oven, warm the oil over medium heat. Add the onion and cook for 4 to 5 minutes, until it starts to soften.
2. Add the lamb and cook for 7 to 8 minutes, stirring so it browns well on all sides.
3. Add the wine. Raise the heat to high and cook for 3 to 4 minutes, until the alcohol in the wine evaporates and the wine reduces by about ⅓.
4. Add the potatoes. Stir well to release any pieces stuck to the bottom of the Dutch oven and cook for 2 minutes. Add the tomato paste diluted in water and 1 teaspoon of the salt.
5. Bring the stew to a boil. Reduce the heat to low, cover, and cook for 1 hour.
6. Uncover the Dutch oven and cook for 5 minutes, until the stew has reached the desired thickness. Adjust the seasoning to taste.
7. Transfer the stew to a serving bowl and serve hot.

Meatballs

I have long thought that the word "meatball" does not begin to capture the deliciousness these bites pack. In Italy, each region and even each town (dare I say, each household) has its own take on meatballs, adding spices, bread, and cheeses to create unique flavors and a memorable taste experience.

And so it goes with Sardinian meatballs. Often, the island's meatballs are served in saffron sauce, a delicacy of Sardinia. This recipe includes greens, which add flavor and keep the meatballs moist and tender. Once you try these delicious creations, you'll never go back to plain meatballs. Pair the meatballs with Cantina Pili Pujades Monica di Sardegna.

YIELD: 4 SERVINGS

FOR THE TOMATO SAUCE:
- 2 tablespoons extra virgin olive oil
- ½ medium onion, chopped (about ¾ cup [113 g])
- 1 (28-ounce [784-g]) can whole tomatoes, chopped
- 1 teaspoon sea salt

FOR THE MEATBALLS:
- 1 bunch beet greens, washed
- 1 quart (948 mL) water
- 2 teaspoons sea salt, divided
- ¾ pound (341 g) lean ground beef
- 3 cloves garlic, finely chopped
- 1 tablespoon chopped fresh parsley
- 2 large eggs
- 2 tablespoons freshly grated pecorino
- ¼ cup (30 g) Homemade Breadcrumbs (see recipe on p. 65)
- ¼ cup (59 mL) extra virgin olive oil

TO MAKE THE TOMATO SAUCE:

1. In a large (6- to 7-quart [5.7- to 6.6-L]) sauté pan, warm the oil over medium-low heat. Add the onion and cook for 7 to 8 minutes, until it softens and becomes translucent.
2. Add the tomatoes and their juice and bring to a boil. Reduce the heat to low, add the salt, and cook for 20 to 30 minutes, until the sauce thickens. Remove from the heat and set aside.

TO MAKE THE MEATBALLS:

3. Remove and discard the beet greens' thick ribs. Chop the green parts into ½-inch (13-mm) strips.
4. In a medium (8- to 12-quart [7.6- to 11.4-L]) stockpot, bring the water and 1 teaspoon of salt to a boil. Add the greens and boil for 3 to 4 minutes, until they are wilted. Remove from the heat. Drain the greens and chop them finely.
5. In a bowl, combine the greens, ground beef, garlic, parsley, eggs, pecorino, breadcrumbs, and 1 teaspoon of salt. Mix with your hands until the mixture is uniform.
6. In a large (6- to 7-quart [5.7- to 6.6-L]) sauté pan, warm the oil over medium-high heat. Add the meatballs, making sure not to overcrowd the pan. Cook until the meatballs are browned on all sides, about 2 minutes per side. Remove from the heat.
7. Add the browned meatballs to the sauté pan containing the tomato sauce. Return to the heat and cook for 5 to 10 minutes.
8. Transfer the meatballs and sauce to a serving bowl and serve hot.

Panadas

This traditional Sardinian dish makes the perfect snack or dinner. Panadas *can be served hot or at room temperature, which makes them a perfect party food.*

Pair with Argiolas Costera, a medium-bodied Cannonau di Sardegna *that perfectly complements the richness of the dish.*

YIELD: 8–12 SERVINGS

FOR THE DOUGH:

- 4½ cups (563 g) all-purpose flour
- ½ teaspoon sea salt
- 3 tablespoons (43 g) chilled butter, cubed
- 3 cups (711 mL) lukewarm water

FOR THE FILLING:

- ¼ cup (59 mL) extra virgin olive oil, plus more, for brushing baking sheets and *Panadas*
- ½ cup (75 g) chopped onion
- ½ cup (60 g) chopped celery
- 1 pound (454 g) lamb, cut into ¼-inch (6-mm) pieces
- 1 bay leaf
- 1½ cups (356 mL) dry red wine
- Sea salt, to taste
- 2 sundried tomatoes, sliced
- 1 clove garlic, minced
- 2 tablespoons fresh parsley, finely chopped
- Pinch saffron
- ½ cup (67 g) chopped green and black olives
- 2 cups (300 g) fresh (or frozen and thawed) fava
- 8 fresh (or frozen and thawed) artichoke hearts, chopped
- ½ teaspoon fresh thyme, finely chopped
- Crushed red pepper, to taste (optional)

RECIPE CONTINUES ON PAGE 212

Panadas (CONTINUED FROM PAGE 211)

TO MAKE THE DOUGH:

1. On a flat, clean working surface, arrange the flour in a mound, add the salt, and make a well in the center. Place the butter in the middle of the well and add a little of the water. Begin incorporating the butter and water into the flour. Very slowly, continue to add the water, kneading to incorporate it into the flour. Continue adding the water, a little at a time, until the dough is soft enough to work, but not sticky. If the dough is sticky, add more flour. If the dough is too dry, add a little more water. Knead for 5 minutes, until the dough is smooth.

2. Wrap the dough in plastic wrap and let it rest on the kitchen counter for at least 30 minutes. (The dough can be made 1 day ahead and refrigerated overnight.)

TO MAKE THE FILLING:

3. In a large (6- to 7-quart [5.7- to 6.6-L]) sauté pan, warm the ¼ cup (59 mL) oil over medium heat. Add the onion and celery and cook for 4 to 5 minutes, until they begin to soften.

4. Add the lamb and bay leaf and cook for 7 to 8 minutes, until the lamb is well browned.

5. Add the wine and cook for 1 minute. Add a pinch of salt. Reduce the heat to low, cover the pan, and cook for 50 minutes.

6. Add the sundried tomatoes, garlic, parsley, saffron, olives, fava, artichokes, thyme, and crushed red pepper (if using) and cook for 20 to 25 minutes, until the meat is tender. Adjust the seasoning to taste. Remove from the heat. Remove and discard the bay leaf.

TO ASSEMBLE THE PANADAS:

7. Preheat the oven to 400°F (200°C).

8. Brush 2 13 × 18-inch (32.5 × 46-cm) baking sheets with part of the remaining oil.

9. Roll out the dough to $1/8$-inch (3-mm) thickness. Cut the dough into circles that are 4 inches (10 cm) in diameter.

10. Place about 1½ tablespoons of the filling in the middle of each circle. Fold the circle to create a half-moon. Press the edges of the dough tightly to close the *Panadas*.

11. Place the *Panadas* on the prepared baking sheets and brush the tops with the rest of the oil. Bake for 35 minutes, until the tops and bottoms of the *Panadas* are golden. Remove from the oven.

12. Transfer to a serving platter and serve warm or at room temperature.

Pork Chops with Olives and *Vernaccia di Oristano*

This dish is simple, quick, and utterly delicious, wowing dinner guests every time. The Vernaccia di Oristano *and olives give the pork a deep, rich flavor. Served with roasted potatoes and endive or broccoli raab, it is a great meal. Pair with Argiolas Iselis Rosso, a delicious blend of monica, carignano, and bovale grapes.*

YIELD: 4 SERVINGS

- 2 tablespoons extra virgin olive oil
- 4 thin-cut pork chops
- 2 cloves garlic, thinly sliced
- 1½ cups (356 mL) Contini Vernaccia di Oristano
- 1 fresh bay leaf
- ½ teaspoon sea salt, plus more, to taste
- ½ cup (67 g) chopped black olives

1. In a sauté pan large enough to accommodate all 4 chops, warm the oil over medium-high heat and brown the pork chops well on both sides, 3 to 4 minutes per side. Add the garlic, stir well, and cook for 1 minute.
2. Add the wine and cook for 4 minutes, until the alcohol evaporates and the wine is reduced by about ⅓.
3. Add the bay leaf and ½ teaspoon of salt. Reduce the heat to low, cover the pan, and cook for 7 to 8 minutes.
4. Add the olives and cook, covered, for 5 minutes. Remove from the heat.
5. Remove the chops from the pan and transfer them to a serving platter. Cover with foil and let them rest for several minutes.
6. Return the pan to the heat. Raise the heat to medium and reduce the wine and olive sauce until it becomes viscous. Remove from the heat. Remove and discard the bay leaf. Adjust the seasoning to taste.
7. Drizzle the chops with the sauce. Serve warm.

Pork Roast with Mediterranean Herbs

One of the most traditional Sardinian dishes is spit-roasted suckling pig (*porcheddu*). It is often flavored with myrtle and other Mediterranean herbs. Since suckling pig is difficult to find, when I am away from Sardinia, I use pork shoulder. The meat is not nearly as tender, but this dish is excellent in winter with a robust red such as Sardus Pater Arruga, a full-bodied Carignano del Sulcis. It is great for entertaining: it can be prepared ahead of time, and it is sure to please your dinner guests.

YIELD: 6 SERVINGS

- 3 pounds (1.36 kg) pork shoulder (or butt) roast
- 5 cloves garlic, sliced
- 2 tablespoons minced fresh sage
- 2 tablespoons minced fresh rosemary
- 1 teaspoon myrtle powder or dried myrtle*
- 2 teaspoons sea salt
- 2 tablespoons extra virgin olive oil
- 1 cup (237 mL) dry white wine

1. Preheat the oven to 425°F (220°C).
2. Cut the pork into at least 2 pieces (to reduce cooking time) and cut 4 to 5 slits into each piece.
3. Combine the garlic, sage, rosemary, and myrtle in a small bowl. Fill the slits with the mixture. Season the pork with the salt.
4. In a large Dutch oven, heat the oil over medium-high heat. Add the roast and brown on all sides, about 5 minutes per side.
5. Add the wine, scrape the brown bits from the bottom of the Dutch oven, cover, and place in the oven for 30 minutes.
6. Reduce the oven temperature to 300°F (150°C) and cook for 1½ to 2 hours, until the pork roast is tender and falls apart. Remove from the oven.
7. Transfer the pork to a deep platter and serve hot.

*Myrtle powder, branches, and leaves are available in many specialty stores.

Spring Lamb with Artichokes

This dish combines two quintessentially Sardinian ingredients: lamb and artichokes. Artichokes grow everywhere in Sardinia and find their way into everything from appetizers to side dishes and savory pies. This dish is the perfect Sunday dinner—easy to prepare and flavorful. Pair with a lighter Carignano del Sulcis*, such as Sardus Pater Is Solus.*

YIELD: 4 SERVINGS

- 2 tablespoons extra virgin olive oil
- 1 pound (454 g) spring lamb, cut into ½-inch (13-cm) cubes
- 2 cloves garlic, minced
- 1 cup (237 mL) dry white wine
- ½ teaspoon sea salt, plus more, to taste
- 12 ounces (341 g) fresh (or frozen and thawed) artichoke hearts

1. In a Dutch oven, warm the oil over medium-high heat. Add the lamb and cook until it is well browned on all sides, about 7 to 9 minutes. Add the garlic and cook for 1 minute, stirring constantly.
2. Add the wine and cook for 3 minutes, until the wine is reduced by ⅓.
3. Add ½ teaspoon of salt. Reduce the heat to low, cover the Dutch oven, and cook for 1 hour.
4. Add the artichokes and stir well. Cover the Dutch oven and cook for 30 to 40 minutes. Adjust the seasoning to taste. Remove from the heat.
5. Transfer the lamb and artichokes to a deep serving platter and serve hot.

Spring Lamb with Fava

This dish is a real spring treat. Fresh fava are one of the first spring vegetables and spring lamb is available in the weeks leading up to Easter. The flavors of this dish are fresh, and the meat is very tender.

Pair with Sardus Pater Is Solus, a smooth and easy-drinking Carignano del Sulcis *with a lot of flavor.*

YIELD: 4 SERVINGS

- 3 tablespoons (15 mL) extra virgin olive oil
- 1 small onion, finely chopped (about ¾ cup [113 g])
- 1 pound (454 g) spring lamb, cut into ½-inch (13-mm) pieces
- 1 cup (237 mL) dry white wine
- ½ teaspoon sea salt plus more, to taste
- 1 bay leaf
- 1 cup (237 mL) water, if needed
- 1 pound (454 g) fresh (or frozen and thawed) fava

1. In a Dutch oven, warm the oil over medium-low heat. Add the onion and cook for 7 to 8 minutes, until it softens and becomes translucent.
2. Add the lamb and cook for 7 to 8 minutes, until it is well browned on all sides.
3. Add the wine and cook for 3 minutes, until the wine reduces by about ⅓.
4. Add ½ teaspoon of the salt and the bay leaf. Stir well. Reduce the heat to low, cover the Dutch oven, and cook for about 45 minutes, until the lamb is tender, adding a little of the water, if necessary.
5. Add the fava, stir well, and cook, uncovered, for 5 minutes. Adjust the seasoning to taste. Remove from the heat.
6. Transfer the lamb and fava to a serving bowl and serve hot.

Tripe Sardinian-Style

Tripe is a traditional dish in many Italian regions. Each region has its own preparation that uses local ingredients. Chef Roberto Flore of Antica Dimora del Gruccione showed me his recipe for tripe, which is quite light and flavorful.

The rich and earthy flavors of the tripe pair well with a full-bodied red wine, such as Sardus Pater Is Arenas.

YIELD: 4–6 SERVINGS

FOR THE TRIPE:
- 1½ pounds (681 g) tripe, cleaned and washed
- 1 cup (237 mL) white wine
- 1 lemon, cut in half
- 1 celery rib, roughly chopped
- 1 onion, roughly chopped
- 2 whole cloves garlic
- 2 bay leaves

FOR THE SAUCE:
- 2 tablespoons extra virgin olive oil
- ½ celery rib, finely chopped
- ½ carrot, finely chopped
- ½ onion, finely chopped
- 1 clove garlic, minced
- 1 bay leaf
- 2 cups (320 g) chopped ripe tomatoes
- 1 tablespoon tomato paste
- 1 teaspoon sea salt, plus more, to taste
- 2 cups (474 mL) water
- Freshly ground black pepper, to taste
- 2 teaspoons julienned mint, for sprinkling
- ¼ cup (25 g) grated *fiore sardo* or other aged smoked cheese, for sprinkling

TO MAKE THE TRIPE:

1. In a medium (8- to 12-quart [7.6- to 11.4-L]) stockpot, combine all of the tripe ingredients. Add water to about 1 inch (2.5 cm) above the ingredients and boil for 1 hour, skimming off any impurities that rise to the surface.
2. Remove from the heat and drain. Let the tripe cool and slice it into thin strips. The tripe can be prepared 1 day ahead of time and refrigerated overnight.

TO MAKE THE SAUCE:

3. In a large (6- to 7-quart [5.7- to 6.6-L]) sauté pan, warm the oil over medium heat. Add the celery, carrot, and onion and cook for 4 to 5 minutes, until the vegetables begin to soften.
4. Add the garlic and bay leaf and cook for 1 minute. Add the tripe and cook for 6 to 7 minutes, until it is well browned.

5. Add the tomatoes, tomato paste, 1 teaspoon of salt, and water and cook for 1½ hours on low heat. Remove from the heat. Remove and discard the bay leaf. Add the black pepper. Adjust the seasoning to taste.

6. Transfer the tripe and sauce to a serving bowl. Serve hot, sprinkled with the mint and cheese.

Veal Meatballs

*My favorite Sardinian chef, Roberto Flore of Antica Dimora del Gruccione, makes the most succulent meatballs. He uses only the meat of the Sardinian red cow (*bue rosso*), which has a lot of flavor. Since* bue rosso *is not available outside of Sardinia, I substitute a tender cut of grassfed veal. It is important not to overwork the meatballs. After you add all the ingredients, simply stir until the mixture is uniform. If you use the meatballs in soups or broths, the trick is to freeze them for a couple of hours, and then add them to the soup while they're still frozen. That way, they don't fall apart.*

YIELD: 6–8 SERVINGS

- 1 pound (454 g) ground grassfed veal
- 1 large egg
- 2 tablespoons breadcrumbs
- ¼ cup (59 mL) milk
- 2 tablespoons freshly grated pecorino
- ½ teaspoon minced dried thyme
- Sea salt and freshly ground black pepper, to taste
- 5 tablespoons (74 mL) extra virgin olive oil, for frying, if necessary

1. Combine all the ingredients, except the oil, in a bowl and mix them together with your hands or a wooden spoon until the mixture is uniform.
2. Using a teaspoon, scoop out each meatball, roll it into a ball with your hands, and place it on a foil-lined baking dish or baking sheet. (At this point, the meatballs can either be cooked or frozen for later use. If you are using the meatballs in soups, add them to the soup while they are still frozen.)
3. In a large (6- to 7-quart [5.7- to 6.6-L]) sauté pan, warm the oil over medium heat. The oil should sizzle when you add the meatballs. Add the meatballs, taking care not to overcrowd the sauté pan. Fry for 4 to 5 minutes, turning to make sure the meatballs are well browned on all sides.
4. Place the cooked meatballs on a serving platter lined with paper towels. Serve hot.

Veal Porterhouse Steaks with *Vernaccia di Oristano*

This recipe is incredibly simple, but the wine gives the meat a wonderful flavor. Veal is naturally tender, and keeping the veal steaks covered in liquid as they cook ensures they stay tender.

The combination of veal and Vernaccia *is heavenly. And, in an unusual twist, this dish pairs perfectly well with the* Vernaccia di Oristano *it is cooked in—odd, as veal normally pairs with red wine.*

I love Contini Vernaccia di Oristano. The wine is aged under flor, *a layer of yeast that floats atop the wine and prevents it from oxidizing. As a result, the wine has an incredibly rich, briny flavor. It's well worth seeking out.*

YIELD: 4 SERVINGS

- 2 tablespoons extra virgin olive oil
- 4 veal porterhouse steaks
- 1½ cups (356 mL) *Vernaccia di Oristano*

1. In a sauté pan large enough to accommodate all 4 steaks, warm the oil over medium-high heat. Add the steaks and brown on both sides, about 3 minutes per side.
2. Add the wine and cook for 2 to 3 minutes, until the alcohol evaporates and the wine has reduced by about ¼.
3. Cover the pan. Reduce the heat to low and cook for 10 to 12 minutes, until the meat is cooked to desired doneness.
4. Remove the steaks from the sauté pan. Transfer them to a platter, cover with foil, and let them rest for at least 5 minutes.
5. In the meantime, continue cooking the wine sauce for 2 to 3 minutes to further reduce it. Remove from the heat.
6. Drizzle the wine sauce on the steaks. Serve hot.

Wild Boar in Red Wine

Wild boar, which is hunted in the island's interior, is very popular in Sardinia. In the winter, you'll see hunters everywhere on the roads of Sardinia, as wild boar is a delicacy particularly appreciated at Christmastime.

Unlike other meats, wild boar is difficult to find in butcher shops, so Sardinians rely on friends and relatives for their yearly supply. Boar is tougher than beef, so marinating it before cooking helps to add flavor and tenderize the meat. If it is cooked over low heat in enough liquid, it will become tender and delicious. Boar has robust flavor, so it is best served with a full-bodied red wine, such as a substantial *Nepente di Oliena* or *Carignano del Sulcis*.

YIELD: 4–6 SERVINGS

FOR THE MARINADE:

- 2 pounds (908 g) wild boar, cut into 1-inch (2.5-cm) cubes
- 1 bottle full-bodied dry red wine such as *Cannonau, Nepente di Oliena*, or *Carignano del Sulcis*
- 2 medium carrots, peeled and cut into ½-inch (13-mm) pieces
- 2 celery ribs, cut into ½-inch (13-mm) pieces
- 2 cloves garlic, minced
- 4 fresh bay leaves
- ⅓ cup (79 mL) red wine vinegar
- ½ teaspoon freshly ground black pepper

FOR THE DISH:

- 3 tablespoons (45 mL) extra virgin olive oil
- 1 medium onion, chopped (about 1½ cups [225 g])
- 4 sundried tomatoes, chopped
- 4 cloves garlic, chopped
- 2 teaspoons sea salt, plus more, to taste
- Freshly ground black pepper, to taste
- Water, as needed
- 1 cup (134 g) green olives (optional)
- ¼ cup (8 g) chopped fresh parsley, for garnish

TO MARINATE THE BOAR:

1. In a large glass bowl, combine the wild boar, wine, carrots, celery, garlic, bay leaves, vinegar, and black pepper. Cover tightly with plastic wrap and refrigerate overnight (at least 8 hours).

2. Remove the wild boar from the marinade and pat it dry with paper towels. Reserve the marinade.

TO PREPARE THE DISH:

3. In a large Dutch oven, warm the oil over medium-high heat. Add the wild boar and brown well on all sides, stirring occasionally, about 10 minutes. Add the onion and cook for 7 to 8 minutes, until the onion is soft and translucent.

4. Add the sundried tomatoes, garlic, 2 teaspoons of salt, and a grind of black pepper and cook for 3 minutes.

5. Add the reserved marinade and cook on high heat for 5 minutes, until the wine reduces by about ⅓.

6. Reduce the heat to low, cover the Dutch oven, and cook for at least 1 hour (and preferably 2), making sure the meat remains covered with liquid. If the wine evaporates, add water. Remove from the heat. Remove and discard the bay leaves. Adjust the seasoning to taste.

7. Add the olives, if desired, and serve hot, garnished with the parsley.

Wild Boar in Sweet and Sour Sauce

Over a lunch of mullet and bottarga *one afternoon, Paolo Contini, a passionate cook and the owner of the Contini winery in Cabras, revealed some of his favorite Sardinian recipes. One of them was this unusual combination of wild boar in a sweet and sour sauce. This traditional Sardinian holiday dish has become a part of my own holiday feasts because of its surprising flavors. Pair with a robust red, such as* Nepente di Oliena *or* Carignano del Sulcis.

YIELD: 6–8 SERVINGS

- ¼ cup (59 mL) extra virgin olive oil
- 1 medium onion, chopped
- ½ cup (8 g) chopped fresh parsley
- 1 teaspoon chopped fresh thyme
- ½ teaspoon dried myrtle leaves*
- 1 clove garlic, minced
- 2 pounds (908 g) wild boar shoulder, cut into 1-inch (2.5-cm) pieces
- 2 teaspoons sea salt, plus more, to taste
- Freshly ground black pepper, to taste
- 3 tablespoons (45 mL) red wine vinegar
- 2 tablespoons granulated sugar
- 1 tablespoon tomato paste, diluted in 2 cups (474 mL) hot water
- Water, as needed

1. In a large Dutch oven, warm the oil over medium heat. Add the onion and cook for 7 to 8 minutes, until it softens and becomes translucent.
2. Add the parsley, thyme, myrtle, and garlic. Stir well and cook for 1 minute.
3. Add the wild boar and brown well on all sides, about 10 minutes, stirring occasionally. Sprinkle with 2 teaspoons of salt and some black pepper.
4. Add the vinegar and cook for 1 minute. Add the sugar, stir well, and cook for 1 minute.
5. Add the tomato paste diluted in water and bring to a boil. Reduce the heat to low, cover the Dutch oven, and cook for 2 to 2½ hours, adding more water, if necessary. Remove from the heat. Adjust the seasoning to taste.
6. Transfer the wild boar and sauce to a serving bowl and serve hot.

*Myrtle branches and leaves are available in many specialty stores.

Contorni (SIDE DISHES)

SARDINIAN SIDE DISHES ARE FLAVORFUL AND imaginative creations based on local ingredients such as fava, artichokes, and fennel. They complete a meal with their lighter, brighter flavors. Meat or seafood might be the star of the show, but Sardinian cooks never neglect to serve *contorni* with a main course.

In fact, some of the dishes in this section are flavorful and rich enough to be meals in their own right, so don't hesitate to serve them on their own!

Baked Artichoke Hearts with Cheese

This rich dish can easily be a meal on its own, especially when paired with Contini Karmis, a rich and intriguing white that is rare among wines—a great pairing with artichokes.

YIELD: 6 SERVINGS

- 1½ quarts (1.42 L) water
- 1½ teaspoons sea salt, plus more, to taste
- 2 cups (340 g) fresh (or frozen and thawed) artichoke hearts
- 1 ounce (28 g) prosciutto, finely chopped (about ¼ cup)
- 1 cup (246 g) fresh whole-milk ricotta
- 1 large egg
- Freshly ground black pepper, to taste
- 2 tablespoons fresh breadcrumbs
- 3 tablespoons (19 g) freshly grated pecorino

1. Preheat the oven to 375°F (190°C).
2. In a medium (8- to 12-quart [7.6- to 11.4-L]) stockpot, bring the water and 1½ teaspoons of salt to a boil. Add the artichoke hearts and boil for 2 minutes. Remove from the heat. Drain.
3. In a medium bowl, combine the prosciutto, ricotta, egg, a pinch of salt, and a grind of black pepper and stir well.
4. In a 9 × 9-inch (22.5 × 22.5-cm) ovenproof baking dish, arrange the artichokes in a single layer. Cover with the ricotta mixture.
5. In a small bowl, combine the breadcrumbs and pecorino and sprinkle over the ricotta.
6. Bake for 30 minutes. Raise the heat to broil and finish under the broiler for 5 minutes, until the top is golden brown. Remove from the oven.
7. Transfer the artichoke hearts to a platter and serve hot.

Baked Eggplant

Eggplant has a rich, almost meaty flavor, which makes this dish a great summer lunch or a complement to simply prepared meats.

YIELD: 4 SERVINGS

- 5 tablespoons (74 mL) extra virgin olive oil, divided
- 1 medium eggplant, sliced into ¼-inch (6-mm) slices
- ½ cup (80 g) chopped fresh tomatoes
- 3 cloves garlic, minced
- Sea salt, to taste
- ¼ cup (8 g) chopped fresh parsley

1. Preheat the oven to 375°F (190°C).
2. Brush the bottom and sides of a 9 × 12-inch (22.5 × 30-cm) ovenproof baking dish with 2 tablespoons of the oil.
3. Arrange the eggplant slices in a single layer. Sprinkle the slices with 1 tablespoon of the tomatoes, ⅓ of the garlic, and a pinch of salt. Drizzle with 1 tablespoon of the oil.
4. Continue layering the eggplant, tomatoes, garlic, and salt, making sure to drizzle 1 tablespoon of oil over each layer, until all ingredients are used.
5. Bake for 1 hour. Remove from the oven, sprinkle with the parsley, transfer to a serving platter, and serve hot.

Endive with Extra Virgin Olive Oil

Endive is a leafy bitter green related to chicory and rich in vitamins and minerals. In the U.S., curly endive is often referred to as chicory. Endive is a common side dish in Sardinia. Its slightly bitter flavor complements rich meat dishes very well. It is most often simply boiled and served with a drizzle of high-quality extra virgin olive oil.

YIELD: 4 SERVINGS

- 2 quarts (1.90 L) water
- 2 teaspoons sea salt, plus more, to taste
- 1 large head of endive, washed and chopped into 1½-inch (3.8-cm) pieces
- Extra virgin olive oil, for drizzling

1. In a medium (8- to 12-quart [7.6- to 11.4-L]) stockpot, bring the water and 2 teaspoons of salt to a boil. Add the endive and cook for 4 to 5 minutes, until it is wilted and dark green in color. Remove from the heat.
2. Drain and transfer to a serving bowl. Adjust the seasoning to taste.
3. Serve warm with a drizzle of excellent extra virgin olive oil.

Fava

Fresh fava are available in spring at farmers' markets and in grocery stores. You can also find frozen fava in most grocery stores. If the fava are bigger, they will need to be peeled. To peel frozen fava, let them thaw and simply slip the green, waxy cover off. To peel fresh fava, first shuck and then remove the outer waxy cover. Either way, fava are a delicious way to add important nutrients to your diet.

YIELD: 4 SERVINGS

> **3 tablespoons (15 mL) extra virgin olive oil**
> **½ medium onion, finely chopped (about ½ cup [75 g])**
> **1 pound (454 g) fresh (or frozen and thawed) fava**
> **Sea salt and freshly ground black pepper, to taste**
> **½ cup (119 mL) water**
> **3 tablespoons (19 g) freshly grated pecorino, for sprinkling (optional)**

1. In a large (6- to 7-quart [5.7- to 6.6-L]) sauté pan, warm the oil over medium heat. Add the onion and cook for 7 to 8 minutes, until it softens and becomes translucent.
2. Add the fava and sprinkle them with the salt and black pepper.
3. Add the water. Reduce the heat to low and cook for 5 to 7 minutes, until the fava are soft. Do not overcook, as the fava will fall apart. Adjust the seasoning to taste.
4. Transfer the fava to a serving bowl and serve hot, sprinkled with the pecorino (if using).

Fava Salad

This salad is the perfect summer lunch or an accompaniment to lighter meats. It is quick and easy to prepare, full of nutrition, and a perfect dish to enjoy at room temperature or cold.

YIELD: 4 SERVINGS

- 3 quarts (2.84 L) water
- 2 teaspoons sea salt, plus more, to taste
- 1½ pounds (681 g) fresh (or frozen and thawed) fava
- 2 cloves garlic, minced
- 2 tablespoons minced fresh parsley
- 3 tablespoons (45 mL) red wine vinegar
- 2 tablespoons extra virgin olive oil
- Crushed red pepper, to taste

1. In a medium (8- to 12-quart [7.6- to 11.4-L]) stockpot, bring the water and 2 teaspoons of salt to a boil. Add the fava and cook for 5 to 7 minutes, until they are soft, but not falling apart. Remove from the heat. Drain and set aside to cool.
2. In a medium bowl, combine the fava, garlic, and parsley. Sprinkle with salt.
3. Add the vinegar, oil, and crushed red pepper. Stir lightly, making sure not to break the fava. Adjust the seasoning to taste.
4. Transfer to a serving bowl and serve at room temperature.

Fava with Pancetta

This rich and satisfying dish is a perfect meal in its own right. It also pairs well with lighter meats.

YIELD: 4 SERVINGS

- 2 tablespoons extra virgin olive oil
- ½ medium onion, finely chopped
- 1 ounce (28 g) pancetta or prosciutto, chopped
- 1 pound (454 g) fresh (or frozen and thawed) fava
- Sea salt and freshly ground black pepper, to taste
- ½ cup (119 mL) water
- 1 tablespoon chopped fresh mint, for sprinkling (optional)

1. In a large (6- to 7-quart [5.7- to 6.6-L]) sauté pan, warm the oil over medium heat. Add the onion and cook for 4 to 5 minutes, until it begins to soften.
2. Add the pancetta or prosciutto and cook for 2 to 3 minutes.
3. Add the fava and sprinkle with salt and black pepper.
4. Add the water. Reduce the heat to low and cook for 5 to 7 minutes, until the fava are done. Remove from the heat. Adjust the seasoning to taste.
5. Transfer the fava to a serving bowl. Serve hot, sprinkled with the mint (if using).

Potatoes and Artichokes

This delicious side dish is the essence of Sardinia. Artichokes are one of the most common vegetables in Sardinia, and they are prepared in many different ways. They give zing and flavor to this dish, which I like to pair with fish and a good Vermentino.

YIELD: 4 SERVINGS

- 6 tablespoons (89 mL) extra virgin olive oil
- 4–5 medium Yukon Gold potatoes (about 800 g), quartered and sliced
- 2 cups (340 g) fresh (or frozen and thawed) artichoke hearts
- 2 cloves garlic, minced
- 1 teaspoon sea salt, plus more, to taste
- 1 tablespoon finely chopped fresh parsley, for sprinkling

1. In a large (6- to 7-quart [5.7- to 6.6-L]) sauté pan, warm the oil over medium-high heat.
2. Add the potatoes in a single layer and cook for 3 to 5 minutes, until the potatoes start to release from the bottom of the pan.
3. Add the artichokes, garlic, and 1 teaspoon of salt. Stir well. Reduce the heat to medium-low, cover, and cook for 25 to 30 minutes, until the potatoes are done. Remove from the heat. Adjust the seasoning to taste.
4. Transfer the potatoes and artichokes to a serving bowl. Sprinkle with the parsley and serve hot.

Potatoes with Fennel and Capers

This dish combines some of the most common Sardinian ingredients: fennel and capers. The fennel gives the dish freshness and an interesting texture, and the salty flavor of the capers perfectly complements the potatoes. This dish goes well with a simple meat dish, such as roasted pork, and a flavorful Sardinian red, such as Carignano del Sulcis.

YIELD: 4 SERVINGS

- 4 medium Yukon Gold potatoes, peeled and cubed
- 1 tablespoon sea salt, divided, plus more, to taste
- 1 gallon (3.80 L) water
- 1 large fennel bulb, cut into quarters and then sliced into ¼-inch (6-mm) slices
- 5 tablespoons (74 mL) extra virgin olive oil
- 1 tablespoon salt-packed capers, chopped
- Freshly ground black pepper, to taste

1. In a medium (8- to 12-quart [7.6- to 11.4-L]) stockpot, cover the potatoes with water to ¾ inch (1.9 cm) above the potatoes. Add ½ tablespoon of salt and bring to a boil. Cook until the potatoes are almost done (you should feel some resistance when you pierce them with a fork). Remove from the heat. Drain and set aside.

2. In another medium (8- to 12-quart [7.6- to 11.4-L]) stockpot, bring the water and the remaining ½ tablespoon of salt to a boil. Add the fennel and cook at a rolling boil for 3 minutes, until the fennel starts to soften but is still crunchy. Remove from the heat. Drain and set aside.

3. In a large (6- to 7-quart [5.7- to 6.6-L]) nonstick sauté pan, warm the oil over medium-high heat. Add the potatoes and cook for 4 to 5 minutes, until they start to brown.

4. Add the fennel and capers and stir well. Cook for 5 to 6 minutes, stirring occasionally to make sure the potatoes and fennel are browning evenly on all sides. Remove from the heat. Add the black pepper. Adjust the seasoning to taste.

5. Transfer to a serving bowl. Serve hot.

Potatoes with Mediterranean Herbs

Once again, a dish becomes truly Sardinian with the addition of Mediterranean herbs like thyme, rosemary, and, of course, myrtle. Pair this dish with any meat dish for a deliciously Sardinian meal.

YIELD: 4 SERVINGS

- **4–5 medium Yukon Gold potatoes (about 800 g), cut into ½-inch (13-mm) cubes**
- **2 teaspoons sea salt, plus more, to taste**
- **½ teaspoon minced fresh rosemary**
- **½ teaspoon minced fresh thyme**
- **½ teaspoon crumbled dried myrtle leaves***
- **¼ cup (59 mL) extra virgin olive oil**
- **Freshly ground black pepper, to taste**

1. Preheat the oven to 375°F (190°C).
2. In a medium (8- to 12-quart [7.6- to 11.4-L]) stockpot, cover the potatoes with water to about ¾ inch (1.9 cm) above the potatoes. Add 2 teaspoons of salt and bring to a boil. Boil the potatoes until they are soft when pierced with a fork but not falling apart. Remove from the heat and drain.
3. In a 9 × 12-inch (22.5 × 30-cm) ovenproof baking dish, distribute the potatoes in a single layer. Sprinkle with the herbs. Drizzle with the oil and stir well, making sure the oil and herbs are evenly distributed. Sprinkle with some salt and black pepper.
4. Bake for at least 45 minutes, until the potatoes are completely done. They should be crunchy on the outside and soft on the inside. Remove from the oven. Adjust the seasoning to taste.
5. Transfer to a serving dish and serve hot.

*Myrtle branches and leaves are available in many specialty stores.

Roasted Tomatoes

This is the perfect summer side dish. When tomatoes are in season, they have lots of flavor, which only becomes more concentrated by roasting them. The Herbed Breadcrumbs add both texture and a depth of flavor.

YIELD: 4 SERVINGS

- 2 large or 4 medium ripe tomatoes
- 4 tablespoons (59 mL) extra virgin olive oil, divided
- 2 cloves garlic, minced
- ¼ cup (30 g) Herbed Breadcrumbs (see recipe on p. 64)
- Sea salt, to taste

1. Preheat the oven to 375°F (190°C).
2. Slice the tomatoes into ¾-inch-thick (1.9-cm-thick) slices. Remove the seeds.
3. Brush a baking sheet with 1 tablespoon of the oil. Place the tomato slices on the baking sheet and distribute the garlic evenly among the slices.
4. Sprinkle with the Herbed Breadcrumbs and salt. Drizzle with the remaining oil.
5. Bake for 45 minutes. Remove from the oven.
6. Transfer the slices to a platter and serve hot or at room temperature.

Sautéed Zucchini

This simple, yet delicious, side dish is perfect as an accompaniment to robust meat dishes, such as Wild Boar in Red Wine (see recipe on p. 222). The pecorino adds richness and complexity to the dish without overpowering it.

YIELD: 4 SERVINGS

- 2 tablespoons extra virgin olive oil
- ½ medium onion, chopped
- 4 small zucchini, cut into halves lengthwise and sliced
- 1 teaspoon sea salt, plus more, to taste
- ½ cup (50 g) freshly grated pecorino, for sprinkling
- ¼ cup (8 g) chopped fresh parsley, for sprinkling

1. In a large (6- to 7-quart [5.7- to 6.6-L]) sauté pan, warm the oil over medium-low heat. Add the onion and cook for 7 to 8 minutes, until it is soft and translucent.

2. Add the zucchini and 1 teaspoon of salt and stir well. Reduce the heat to low, cover, and cook for 10 minutes, until the zucchini soften. Remove from the heat. Adjust the seasoning to taste.

3. Serve hot or at room temperature, sprinkled with the pecorino and parsley.

Zucchini Salad with Tomatoes and Cheese

This light salad is full of flavor and pairs well with meat or a rich pasta dish. In this dish, Sardinian cooks traditionally use a young, slightly acidic type of cheese that's not available in North America. I substitute cow's-milk feta cheese, which has a similar flavor.

YIELD: 4 SERVINGS

- 3 tablespoons (45 mL) extra virgin olive oil
- ½ small red onion, thinly sliced (about ½ cup [75 g])
- 2 medium zucchini, cut lengthwise into quarters and sliced into ⅛-inch-thick (3-mm-thick) slices
- Sea salt, to taste
- 1 ripe tomato, seeded and chopped
- ¼ cup (38 g) crumbled cow's-milk feta cheese, for sprinkling
- ½ teaspoon chopped fresh basil, for sprinkling

1. In a small (2- to 3-quart [1.9- to 2.8-L]) sauté pan, warm the oil over medium-low heat. Add the onion and cook for 7 to 8 minutes, until it softens and becomes translucent.
2. Add the zucchini and a pinch of salt and stir well. Cover and cook for 8 minutes, until the zucchini are cooked, but still slightly crunchy on the inside. Remove from the heat.
3. Transfer to a serving bowl. Add the tomato. Stir well. Sprinkle with the feta cheese and basil. Adjust the seasoning to taste and serve warm or at room temperature.

Dolci (DESSERTS)

SARDINIAN DESSERTS ARE CLOSELY TIED TO RELIGIOUS holidays and other celebrations. In the past, when much of the island was plagued by poverty, desserts were not an everyday delicacy as they are today.

The most famous Sardinian dessert is undoubtedly the *sebada*, a fried dough pocket filled with cheese and drizzled with bitter honey. Another common sweet are *amaretti*, chewy almond cookies that come in many varieties. Sardinia is also famous for *torrone* (nougat), the best of which is made with honey and has an enchanting flavor.

Each town in Sardinia has its own sweets. Some are variations on a theme you can find most anywhere on the island; others are unique creations confined to a small area.

In the southern portion of the island, the Arab influence is very strong, so flavors like orange blossom, cinnamon, and vanilla are common. This influence decreases gradually as you move north, where many desserts include cooked grape must.

The cheese used in desserts also varies. In the south, ricotta is more common, while in the center of the island, pecorino takes over. Not surprisingly, cheese desserts from the center of the island have a much stronger flavor.

One unique ingredient in Sardinian sweets is *sapa*, the juice obtained from the first pressing of grapes that is then cooked down to a thick syrup. Cooking *sapa* can take the better part of a day. Once the cooked must has rested overnight, it can be poured into bottles and jars and preserved for long periods of time. Many Sardinian wineries bottle and sell *sapa*. Look for it—it's an ingredient worth seeking out.

Almond and Orange Brittle (*Aranzada*)

This sweet treat, which is typically prepared for wedding celebrations, embodies the food culture of the island. It is simple to prepare and uses orange peel that would otherwise go to waste. It is also long lasting, so it can be prepared well in advance. Traditionally, it was found in the interior, around Nuoro, but today you can find it in pastry shops all over Sardinia. It makes an excellent afternoon snack, as it gives long-lasting energy.

YIELD: 6–8 SERVINGS

- 2 oranges, peels removed, cleaned of pith and thinly sliced
- ½ cup (119 mL) honey
- ½ cup (54 g) slivered almonds, lightly toasted

1. Soak the orange peels in cold water for at least 2 days. Drain well, pressing them to get rid of any excess water. Set aside.
2. Line an 8.5 × 5-inch (21.5 × 12.5-cm) loaf pan with foil.
3. In a small (2- to 3-quart [1.9- to 2.8-L]) nonstick sauté pan, cook the orange peels with the honey for 20 minutes, stirring occasionally, until the honey has been absorbed.
4. Add the almonds and cook for 2 minutes, until almonds are incorporated into the mixture. Remove from the heat.
5. Distribute the mixture evenly into the prepared loaf pan and let cool.
6. Cut into 1-inch (2.5-cm) squares and serve. This dessert can be prepared 2 to 3 days ahead of time and stored in an airtight container at room temperature.

Amarettus (Amaretti)

These simple cookies are one of the most satisfying Sardinian desserts. They are rich, yet light, full of flavor, and a perfect complement to coffee or tea.

YIELD: 25–30 COOKIES

- 2 cups (200 g) ground almonds or almond meal
- 1 cup (225 g) granulated sugar
- 3 large egg whites
- 1 teaspoon vanilla
- ½ teaspoon almond extract

1. Line 2 11 × 17-inch (27.5 × 43-cm) baking sheets with parchment paper.
2. In a medium bowl, combine the almonds and sugar and stir well. Set aside.
3. In another medium bowl, beat the egg whites to stiff peaks. Set aside.
4. Fold the almonds and sugar into the egg whites. Add the vanilla and almond extract and stir slowly, until the mixture is uniform.
5. Using a teaspoon, scoop and drop the cookies onto the prepared baking sheets. Let the cookies rest for 1 to 2 hours at room temperature before baking.
6. Preheat the oven to 250°F (120°C).
7. Bake for 1 hour, until the cookies are firm to the touch. Remove from the oven.
8. Let the cookies cool slightly on a wire rack and transfer to a serving platter. Serve warm or at room temperature.

Butter Cookies

This is the Sardinian version of shortbread. The cookies are lighter than regular shortbread, but full of flavor. They're simply irresistible!

YIELD: 30–40 COOKIES

- 3½ cups (438 g) all-purpose flour
- 2 teaspoons baking powder
- 5 large egg yolks
- 1⅛ cups (253 g) granulated sugar
- 7 tablespoons (100 g) butter, melted
- Zest of 1 lemon

1. In a medium bowl, combine the flour and baking powder.
2. In a large bowl, whisk the egg yolks and sugar until the mixture is thick and pale.
3. Add the melted butter and stir well. Slowly add the flour and baking powder mixture, stirring constantly.
4. Add the lemon zest. Continue mixing until all ingredients are well combined and a workable dough forms.
5. Remove the dough from the bowl and knead on a clean surface for 1 to 2 minutes, until it is smooth and comes together. Form the dough into a disk. Wrap the dough in plastic wrap and refrigerate for at least 3 hours or up to 2 days.
6. Preheat the oven to 375°F (190°C).
7. Line 2 11 × 17-inch (27.5 × 43-cm) baking sheets with parchment paper.
8. Roll out the dough to ¼-inch (6-mm) thickness and cut using cookie cutters. Place the cookies on the prepared baking sheets.
9. Bake for 30 to 40 minutes, until golden brown. Remove from the oven.
10. Let the cookies cool slightly on a wire rack and transfer to a serving platter. Serve warm or at room temperature.

Chocolate *Mirto* Truffles

The traditional Sardinian liqueur mirto *has a rich and unique flavor that never fails to remind me of the island. After my first taste of* mirto*, I had the idea to pair it with chocolate.*

This recipe developed out of that idea. It is not a traditional Sardinian recipe, but everyone I've shared these truffles with has loved them so much that I couldn't help but include the recipe in this collection.

YIELD: 16–20 TRUFFLES

- **10 ounces (284 g) dark chocolate (69%–75% cacao)**
- **6 tablespoons (85 g) butter**
- **2 tablespoons *mirto* liqueur**
- **¼ cup (22 g) unsweetened cocoa powder**

1. Line an 8.5 × 5-inch (21.5 × 12.5-cm) loaf pan with foil.
2. In a double boiler, melt the chocolate and butter over low heat, stirring occasionally. Remove from the heat.
3. Off the heat, add the *mirto*. Stir well and pour into the prepared loaf pan.
4. Cool the chocolate at room temperature until it becomes firm, at least 1 hour.
5. Scoop the chocolate using a melon baller or teaspoon. Roll the chocolate pieces into balls quickly with your hands, smoothing out any edges. The truffles are supposed to be rustic, so don't roll them until they are completely smooth.
6. Roll the truffles in the cocoa powder and place them on parchment paper. Store in an airtight container in the refrigerator. Remove from the refrigerator about 30 minutes before serving.

Note: The truffles can be made 2 to 3 days ahead of time, but they're best when fresh.

Crema Catalana

Crema Catalana, which is Spanish in origin, is a common dessert in the town of Alghero. Alghero's culture and cuisine boast many Catalan influences. This recipe was given to me by Vittoria, the co-owner of my favorite restaurant in Alghero, Trattoria Cavour (now Trattoria Lo Romani).

YIELD: 8 SERVINGS

- 3½ cups (830 mL) whole milk
- 1 cup (237 mL) heavy cream
- ½ teaspoon lemon zest
- Pinch ground cinnamon
- 6 large egg yolks
- 1 cup (225 g) granulated sugar, plus more, for sprinkling
- 5 tablespoons (39 g) all-purpose flour

1. In a medium (2- to 3-quart [1.9- to 2.8-L]) saucepan, combine the milk, cream, lemon zest, and cinnamon. Warm on low heat, making sure the mixture does not come to a boil. Remove from the heat and set aside.
2. In the meantime, in a large bowl, beat the egg yolks and sugar until thick and pale. Add the flour, 1 tablespoon at a time, making sure each tablespoon has been completely incorporated before adding more.
3. Start adding the milk mixture to the egg mixture, 1 ladle at a time. Doing so gradually warms the eggs without cooking them through.
4. Transfer the combined mixture to the saucepan. Stir well. Cook on low heat for 5 to 7 minutes, until the mixture starts to thicken.
5. Remove from the heat. Divide into 8 ramekins. Cool and refrigerate until ready to serve, up to 3 days.
6. Sprinkle a little sugar on the surface of each ramekin and caramelize it with a kitchen blowtorch. If you do not have a torch, turn on the broiler and finish the ramekins under the broiler for 2 to 3 minutes, until the tops are hard and golden brown. Remove from the oven.
7. Serve warm in the ramekins.

Fig Tart with *Sapa*

This tart is Sardinian to its core: It features fresh figs, one of the most common fruits on this Mediterranean island, and sapa, *a cooked grape must, which often finds its way into Sardinian desserts. Of course, since it is made with Moscato, the tart also pairs perfectly with a sweet Moscato.*

YIELD: 8–12 SERVINGS

FOR THE CRUST:
- ¾ cup (169 g) granulated sugar
- 1 large egg
- 2¾ cups (344 g) all-purpose flour
- ⅓ cup (79 mL) Moscato (sweet white wine)
- 1 stick (114 g) butter, softened

FOR THE TART:
- 1 tablespoon extra virgin olive oil
- All-purpose flour, for rolling dough
- 18 ripe fresh figs, peeled and slightly mashed
- ¼ cup (59 mL) *sapa*

TO MAKE THE CRUST:

1. In the bowl of a stand mixer, beat the sugar and egg on medium speed until creamy. Slowly add the flour and wine, beating constantly at low speed.
2. Add the butter and continue beating until the dough is uniform. Remove the dough from the mixer bowl. Wrap in plastic wrap and refrigerate for at least 20 minutes.

TO MAKE THE TART:

3. Preheat the oven to 375°F (190°C). Brush the bottom and sides of a 10-inch (25-cm) tart pan with the oil.
4. Separate the dough into 2 pieces, 1 about 50% larger than the other. On a floured surface, roll out the bigger piece of dough to ¼-inch (6-mm) thickness, adding some flour to prevent the dough from sticking.
5. Line the prepared tart pan with the dough, cutting off any excess parts.
6. Layer the figs on the bottom round of dough and sprinkle with the *sapa*.
7. Roll out the smaller piece of dough to ¼-inch (6-mm) thickness. Cover the figs with the smaller piece of dough and press the edges of dough to close.
8. Bake for 35 to 40 minutes, until the top and bottom of the tart are browned. Remove from the oven. Set aside to cool slightly.
9. Remove from the tart pan and transfer to a serving platter. Serve warm or at room temperature.

Pardulas

In Sardinia's past, sweets were reserved for special occasions, such as weddings, birthdays, and saints' days. *Pardulas* were traditionally made for Easter in southern Sardinia. Today, you can find them in Sardinia's pastry shops and kitchens year round.

YIELD: 12 SERVINGS

FOR THE DOUGH:

- ⅝ cup (88 g) *semola rimacinata**
- 1 tablespoon butter or extra virgin olive oil
- 1 large egg
- Sea salt, to taste
- Cold water, as needed

FOR THE FILLING:

- 1 pound (454 g) fresh ricotta**
- ¼ cup (56 g) granulated sugar
- 2 tablespoons all-purpose flour
- 1 large egg, plus another large egg yolk, for brushing
- Zest of 1 lemon
- Pinch saffron

TO MAKE THE DOUGH:

1. In a medium bowl, combine the *semola rimacinata*, butter or oil, egg, and salt. Stir slowly, integrating the fat and egg into the flour.
2. Add enough water to create a firm dough. Knead until the dough comes together. (The dough can also be made in a stand mixer or a food processor.)
3. Wrap the dough in plastic wrap and let it rest in a cool place for at least 20 minutes.

TO MAKE THE FILLING:

4. In a medium bowl, combine the ricotta, sugar, flour, whole egg, lemon zest, and saffron. Stir well. Set aside.

TO ASSEMBLE THE *PARDULAS*:

5. Preheat the oven to 375°F (190°C). Line an 11 × 17-inch (27.5 × 43-cm) baking sheet with parchment paper.
6. Roll out the dough to ⅛-inch (3-mm) thickness. Cut 12 4-inch (10-cm) circles out of the dough using a water glass or a round cookie cutter.

7. Place 1 heaping tablespoon of filling in the center of each circle, leaving about ¼ inch (6 mm) of dough around the filling. Lift up the edges of the dough and pinch the edges in several places around the filling, creating a cup.

8. Place the filled dough cups on the prepared baking sheet. Brush the tops with the egg yolk.

9. Bake for 30 minutes.

10. Raise the heat to broil. Finish under the broiler for 3 to 4 minutes, until the tops are golden brown. Remove from the oven.

11. Let the *Pardulas* cool and then transfer to a serving platter. Serve with *Malvasia* or another sweet wine.

*Semola rimacinata *is finely ground semolina (durum wheat) flour. If you cannot find* semola rimacinata, *use ½ regular semolina flour and ½ all-purpose flour.*

**In Sardinia, it is traditional to use a very young cheese (1- or 2-day-old pecorino cheese) in this dish.*

Pecorino with Honey

This is one of the simplest, yet most delicious, of all Sardinian desserts. It includes two very traditional Sardinian products: pecorino, which is found on every table in Sardinia, and honey, which comes in many varieties and expresses the characteristics of the area it came from and the flowers the bees fed on.

Pecorino can make a cheese lover out of the most dedicated vegan. Once you taste Sardinian honey, you'll understand that the differences between the honey yielded from chestnut, orange, and artichoke pollen are not trivial. The vastly different types of honey pair well with very different foods. For this dish, I like to use a more robust honey, such as chestnut or cardoon. I leave the flowery honeys for other sweets.

YIELD: 4 SERVINGS

- 4 ounces (114 g) high-quality pecorino, preferably not aged more than 3 months
- 4–6 tablespoons (59–89 mL) Sardinian chestnut or cardoon honey

1. Preheat the oven to broil.
2. Slice the pecorino into 4 slices and place them in an ovenproof baking dish big enough to handle all 4 slices.
3. Melt the pecorino under the broiler for 5 to 6 minutes, until it is soft, but not burnt. Remove from the oven.
4. Divide the melted pecorino among 4 plates. Serve hot, drizzled with the honey.

Raisin Cookies (*Pabassinos* or *Papassinus*)

These cookies come in many different variations from south to north. Typically prepared for fall and winter holidays, their name derives from pabassa, *the Sardinian word for raisin. Sometimes, they also contain fennel seeds, the flavor of which pairs well with the raisins and lemon zest. The cookies are traditionally shaped like rhomboids, but I have simplified the recipe by making them round.*

YIELD: 35–45 COOKIES

FOR THE COOKIES:
- 1¾ cups (219 g) all-purpose flour
- 1 stick plus 2 tablespoons (142 g) butter, at room temperature
- ¾ cup (169 g) granulated sugar
- 2 large eggs
- ¾ cup (124 g) raisins, soaked in warm water for 10 minutes and drained
- ½ cup (54 g) chopped toasted almonds
- ⅓ cup (38 g) chopped walnuts
- Zest of 1 lemon
- Sea salt, to taste

FOR THE GLAZE:
- 1 cup (100 g) confectioners' sugar
- Juice of 1 lemon
- Water, if needed

TO MAKE THE COOKIES:

1. In a large bowl, combine the flour, butter, sugar, eggs, raisins, almonds, walnuts, lemon zest, and a pinch of salt. Stir until the mixture is uniform and forms into a dough.
2. On a clean, flat surface, roll the dough into logs about 1½ inches (3.8 cm) in diameter. Wrap in plastic wrap and refrigerate for 20 to 30 minutes.
3. Preheat the oven to 375°F (190°C). Line 2 11 × 17-inch (27.5 × 43-cm) baking sheets with parchment paper.

RECIPE CONTINUES ON PAGE 256

Raisin Cookies (*Pabassinos* or *Papassinus*)

(CONTINUED FROM PAGE 255)

4. Cut the dough into ¼-inch-thick (6-mm-thick) cookies. Place the cookies on the prepared baking sheets, ½ inch (13 mm) apart. Bake for 25 to 28 minutes, until the cookies are golden brown. Remove from the oven. Lower the oven temperature to 200°F (93°C).

TO MAKE THE GLAZE:

5. While the dough is baking, stir together the confectioners' sugar and lemon juice until the mixture is uniform, adding a little water, if necessary.
6. Spread the glaze on the cooled cookies. Bake for 10 minutes. Remove from the oven.
7. Let the cookies cool slightly on a wire rack and transfer to a serving platter. Serve warm or at room temperature. The cookies can be stored in an airtight container for up to 5 days.

Ricotta Cake

This flavorful, not-too-sweet cake is perfect as an afternoon snack or a dessert after a light meal. Use the best-quality ricotta you can find, and never substitute lowfat ricotta.

YIELD: 12 SERVINGS

- 1 tablespoon extra virgin olive oil, for brushing
- 1½ cups (338 g) granulated sugar
- 1¼ cups (300 g) ricotta, preferably sheep's milk
- Pinch saffron
- 4 large egg yolks
- Zest of 1 orange
- 2⅓ cups (292 g) all-purpose flour
- 1 teaspoon baking powder
- 2 tablespoons confectioners' sugar, for sprinkling

1. Preheat the oven to 375°F (190°C). Brush the bottom and sides of a 10-inch (25-cm) springform pan with the oil.
2. In a medium bowl, beat the sugar, ricotta, and saffron with an electric mixer for 2 to 3 minutes.
3. Add the egg yolks and continue beating for 2 to 3 minutes on medium speed. Add the orange zest and stir well.
4. In another medium bowl, combine the flour and baking powder. Slowly add the dry ingredients into the wet ingredients in thirds, stirring constantly.
5. Pour the batter into the prepared springform pan.
6. Bake for 35 to 40 minutes, until a toothpick inserted in the center comes out clean. Remove from the oven and let cool.
7. Remove the cake from the springform pan and transfer to a serving platter. Sprinkle with the confectioners' sugar and serve at room temperature.

Sebadas (or Seadas)

Sebadas, *the most traditional of all Sardinian desserts, barely need explanation. They are the first sweet that most who journey to Sardinia will encounter. Like any food that has been around for a long time,* sebadas *come in many variations, but the principle is always the same: A pasta-like dough is filled with cheese, fried, and drizzled with bitter honey. It's heaven on a plate!*

YIELD: 6 SERVINGS

- 14 ounces (397 g) young pecorino, grated*
- 1½ cups (356 mL) lukewarm water, divided, plus more, as needed
- 1 tablespoon semolina flour
- Zest of ½ lemon
- 4 cups (500 g) all-purpose flour
- 2 ounces (57 g) butter or lard
- Sea salt, to taste
- 1½ quarts (1.42 L) extra virgin olive oil, for frying
- ½ cup (119 mL) bitter Sardinian honey (*miele di corbezzolo*)

1. In a medium (2- to 3-quart [1.9- to 2.8-L]) saucepan, combine the pecorino, 1 cup (237 mL) lukewarm water, semolina flour, and lemon zest. Warm the mixture over medium heat, stirring constantly until it is uniform in texture.
2. Spread the mixture on a clean dry surface (such as a chopping block) to a ½-inch (13-mm) thickness. Let it cool until it reaches room temperature and is firm.
3. On a flat working surface, arrange the flour and a pinch of salt or more to taste in a mound. Make a crater in the center of the mound and place the butter or lard in the crater. Add a little of the remaining lukewarm water and start incorporating the butter and water into the flour. Slowly continue to add the water until the dough comes together and is not sticky. If the dough is too dry and tears, add a little water. If the dough is too wet and sticks, add more flour. Knead for 10 minutes, until the dough is smooth.
4. Wrap the dough in plastic wrap and let rest for at least 20 minutes.
5. Roll the dough out to an ⅛-inch (3-mm) thickness and cut it into 12 3- to 4-inch (7.5- to 10-cm) circles.
6. Cut the cooled pecorino into pieces that fit onto the circles of dough. Place the pecorino on half of the dough circles, leaving about ½ inch (13 mm) of dough on all sides.
7. Cover each piece of dough and pecorino with another circle of dough, pinching the edges to close the *sebadas* tightly.

8. In a large (6- to 7-quart [5.7- to 6.6-L]) sauté pan at least 3 inches (7.5 cm) deep, warm the oil. The oil should be hot, but not smoking (200°F to 210°F [93°C to 99°C]).

9. Fry the *sebadas* several at a time, making sure not to overcrowd the pan. The *sebadas* should always sizzle while they're frying. After 7 to 9 minutes, when the *sebadas* are golden brown, remove them from the pan and place them on a platter lined with paper towels. Let them rest for 5 minutes.

10. Serve the *sebadas* on individual plates, drizzled with the honey. Serve hot.

Use the youngest pecorino possible, as it needs to be soft and must melt easily.

Sources

It seems like every day, Sardinian products are becoming more widely available in the U.S. Here are some of my favorite sources for products:

- **Academia Barilla** (www.academiabarilla.com): The organization's website is an excellent source of Sardinian pecorino cheese (both *dolce* and *gran cru*) and also a wonderful resource for other Italian products, including parmigiano–reggiano cheese, *prosciutto di Parma*, high-quality extra virgin olive oil, canned cherry tomatoes, *aceto balsamico tradizionale di Modena*, and a number of artisanal compotes.
- **Buon Gusto Market** (www.buongustomarket.com): Importer of excellent Sardinian wines and cheeses.
- **Eataly** (www.eataly.com): an Italian food and wine emporium offering authentic ingredients.
- **Gourmet Sardinia** (www.gourmetsardinia.com): Importer of a variety of Sardinian products, including *pane carasau, sapa, fregola*, extra virgin olive oil, and wine.
- **Mint Creek Farm** (www.mintcreekfarm.com): A family farm in Illinois that raises a variety of premium, grassfed meats, including lamb.

Acknowledgments

My deepest gratitude goes to all of my Sardinian friends and contacts who generously shared their stories and recipes and made this book possible. I do want to extend special thanks to those who I worked with most closely:

- Mario Delitala of Motus in Sardinia introduced me to his extraordinary mother, Editta Costa, who generously invited me into her kitchen and taught me much about Sardinian cooking. Editta shared her family's recipes and asked her friends to do the same. Her generosity and energy are boundless. As I cooked with her, I got to know the real Sardinia. Editta's entire family, from her husband Marcello to her granddaughter Delia, regaled me with stories about Sardinian food, traditions, and flavors. The moments spent with them remain some of my most treasured memories of the island.

- My deepest gratitude goes to Giorgio Congiu, a great friend and fascinating storyteller who not only helped us learn about the history and archaeology of the island, but also introduced us to life in the interior. He made introductions to friends and neighbors, who generously welcomed us into their homes and shared their food, stories, and recipes.

- I appreciate the kindness of James Grove, Sara Pisci, and Sara's extended family—especially her aunt, Mariella Pisci, who generously shared her knowledge of the customs of the island.

- I give special thanks to Gabriella Belloni, Lucilla Speciale, and Roberto Flore of the hotel and restaurant Antica Dimora del Gruccione. Roberto generously shared many of his delicious recipes and showed me the true richness of Sardinian cuisine. Roberto, Lucilla, and Gabriella welcomed us warmly at Antica Dimora del Gruccione and told me much about the area of Montiferru and its traditions. Antica Dimora del Gruccione remains one of my most treasured memories and Roberto's food is a constant temptation to go back to Sardinia.
- Carla Marcis taught me how to make *fregola* and cook with it.
- Giulia Annis introduced me to the endless food and wine treasures of Sardinia and patiently answered my many questions.
- Valentina and Antonio Argiolas helped me get to know their family's winery and wines.
- Paolo Contini gave me a wonderful introduction not only to his winery, but also to the entire Cabras/Oristano area. I'll never forget how he mobilized his friends to show me the real Sardinia from the *bottarga* of Cabras to the *lorighitas* of Morgongiori.
- Antonella Chessa, her brother Beppe, and her extraordinary mother Maria Teresa of Su Barchile in Orosei welcomed me like family and shared the foods and wines of their area.
- Vittoria and Gigi of Trattoria Cavour (now Trattoria Lo Romani) in Alghero became instant friends the first time I entered their restaurant. They generously shared their traditions.

- Signora Pasqua of Su Gologone showed me the bounty of Oliena and treated me to some unforgettable foods.
- Claudio Falchi helped me learn about Marghine and patiently explained authentic Sardinian products at length.
- Marco Ligabue shared with me his favorite places in Alghero.
- Kim Sayid of Academia Barilla introduced me to Latteria Sociale Cooperativa San Pasquale in Nulvi, the producers of Academia Barilla pecorino. The Cooperativa allowed me to witness the fascinating process of making different types of pecorino, a true Sardinian treasure. The visit gave me a new appreciation for pecorino.
- Fabio Pibiri introduced me to wonderful Sardinian wines in Chicago. His work is invaluable for the U.S. market.
- Most of all, I am grateful to my husband, photographer, and fellow adventurer Michael Potts, the best travel and production crew a writer could wish for. His patience and adventurous spirit made being far away from home for long periods bearable and (dare I say it?) fun. Michael and my Chicago friends also fearlessly taste-tested all the recipes in this book and offered valuable feedback.
- Thanks too to the dedicated Agate Publishing team, under the leadership of Doug Seibold, for believing in this book and wanting to explore with me the lesser known regions of Italy.

Any and all mistakes in the book are, of course, mine alone.

Index

A

Almond and Orange Brittle (*Aranzada*), 244
Amarettus (*Amaretti*), 246
Artichok(es)
    Baked with Cheese, 227
    with *Bottarga*, 56
    Soup, 152
Asparagus
    Wild, 134
    Risotto with, 135
    Spaghetti with Wild Asparagus, 147
    Soup, 154-5

B

Baccalà with Tomatoes, Olives, and Wild Fennel, 181
Barbagia, 23
Bass
    Striped with Vegetables, 191
Bean(s)
    and Cabbage Soup, 157
    Garbanzo Soup with Wild Fennel, 164
    Minestrone with Garbanzo, 171
    Soup, 156
Bottarga, 36, 45, 52,
    Artichokes with, 56
    Corkscrew-shaped Pasta with Zucchini Cream and, 94-5
    Mullet, 67
    Risotto with, 133
    Spaghetti with, 138
    Tomato Bruschetta with, 81
Bread
    Fainé, 41
    Focaccia Sarda, 60-61
    Pane carasau, 40
        with Olive Oil and Seasalt, 74
        with Pecorino, 73
    Pane civraxiu, 41
    Pane frattau, 118-9
    Pane guttiau, 41
    Pane pistoccu, 41
    Pane spianada (*spianata*), 41
Breadcrumbs
    Herbed, 64
    Homemade, 65
Burrida
    Cagliari-style, 57
    Oristano-style, 58

C

Calamari Stew, 182
Campidano, 25
Cheese
    Casizolu, 33, 44
    Casu marzu, 44
    Fiore sardo, 42, 43
    Pecorino with honey, 254
    Pecorino gran cru, 43, 44
    Pecorino romano, 42, 43
    Pecorino sardo, 42
        dolce, 42-43
        maturo, 43
Chicken
    Braised with Myrtle and Red Wine, 194
    with Capers, 195
    Lorighitas with Free-Range Chicken, 108-9
    with Tomatoes and Olives, 196
    with *Vernaccia di Oristano*, 197
Clams
    Spaghetti with, 141

Cookies
    Butter, 247
    Pardulas, 252-3
    Raisin, 256-6
Cordula, 202
Costa Smeralda (Emerald Coast), 22
Couscous with Vegetables, 96-97
Crema Catalana, 250
Crushed red pepper
    Spaghetti with, 142

E

Eggplant, Baked, 228
Eggs
    Deviled, 59
    Sweet Pea Frittata, 80

Endive with Extra Virgin Olive Oil, 229
Extra Virgin Olive Oil, 46

F

Fava, 62, 230
    Fresh with Mint, 63
    Minestrone with, 168
    with Pancetta, 233
    and Pork Stew (*Favata*), 160
    Raw, Fresh with Olive Oil, 76
    Salad, 232
Fennel
    Wild, 120
    Penne with Wild Fennel and Pancetta, 121
    Soup, 161-2

Fish in Salt Crust, 184
Fregola
    Baked with Pecorino, 90
    Beet Green and Fregola Soup (*Lampazzu*), 158
    in Cheese Broth (*Fregola in Brodo*), 163
    with Clams, 101
    with Sausage and Pecorino, 102

G

Gallura, 23
Gennargentu, 25

Grapes
- bovale sardo, 52
- cagnulari, 52
- cannonau, 49, 51
- carignano, 51
- monica, 51
- nasco, 51
- torbato, 51
- vermentino, 49

H

Honey, 46
- Pecorino with, 254

L

Lentil Soup with Potatoes and Beets, 167

Lobster
- *alla Catalana*, 35-6
- Linguine with, 106-7

M

Malloreddus (*Gnocchetti Sardi*), 110
- *alla Campidanese* (with Sausage), 116
- with Fresh Fava and Pecorino, 113
- with Meat Sauce, 114
- with Young Pecorino, 115

Meat
- Baked Semolina Gnocchi with Meat Sauce, 92-3
- *Bue rosso*, 33
- Goat, 34
  - with Wild Fennel, 201
- Lamb, 32
  - with Fennel and Sundried Tomatoes, 206
  - Spring Lamb with Artichokes, 215
  - Spring Lamb with Fava, 217
  - Stew, 205
  - Stew with Potatoes, 207
- Meatballs, 208-9
- Mini Meatballs, 66-67
- Porcheddu, 34, 199
- Pork
  - Chops with Olives and *Vernaccia di Oristano*, 213
  - Roast with Mediterranean Herbs, 214
- Sausage, 34
- Spit-roasting, 32
- Veal Meatballs, 220
- Veal Porterhouse Steaks with *Vernaccia di Oristano*, 221
- Wild Boar, 34, 199
  - in Red Wine, 222-223
  - Rigatoni with, 131-2
  - in Sweet and Sour Sauce, 225

Mirto, 26, 53
- Chocolate *Mirto* Truffles, 248

Murales, 25, 30

Mussels
- in Spicy Tomato Sauce, 188
- Steamed, 79

N

Nuraghi, 27

O

Octopus
- with Celery, 71
- Potato, and Green Bean Salad, 187
- in Tomato and Garlic Sauce (*Agliata*), 69-70

Olives, Marinated, 65

P

Panadas, 211-2

Peas
    Pea Soup with Pasta and Ricotta, 173

Potatoes
    and Artichokes, 235
    with Fennel and Capers, 236
    with Mediterranean Herbs, 237

R

Ravioli
    with Eggplant and Sausage, 130
    Potato and Mint, 122-3
    Potato and Mint in Tomato Sauce, 124
    Potato and Mint with Lamb Ragù, 125
    Ricotta and Greens, 126-7
    Ricotta and Greens with Wild Fennel, 128-9

Ricotta, 44
    Cake, 257

S

Saffron, 47

Sanguinaccio (Blood Sausage), 200

Sappa, 243
    Fig Tart with, 251

Sardines
    Grilled, 185
    with Lemon, Garlic, and Parsley, 189

Sardo, 29

Sea Bream with Red Onion, 190

Seafood
    Pasta, 137
    Soup, 174

Sebadas, 258-9

Shrimp Salad, 77

Swordfish with Peas, 192

T

Tomatoes
    Roasted, 238
    Sundried, 47

Tripe Sardinian-Style, 218-9

Tuna
    Fettucine with Olives, Capers, and Tuna, 99
    Lasagne with Tuna and Pesto, 104-5
    Spaghetti with Tuna and Olives, 144

V

Vegetables
    Couscous with, 96-7
    Fritters, 82
    Panada, 84-5

W

Walnuts
    Tagliatelle with, 149

Z

Zucchini
    Salad with Tomatoes and Cheese, 240
    Sauteed, 239
    Soup with *Fregola*, 177
    Spaghetti with Zucchini and *Vernaccia di Oristano*, 148

Zuppa Gallurese (*Zuppa Quatta*), 151, 178

About the Author

Viktorija Todorovska is a cookbook author and food and wine instructor. Passionate about the cooking and wines of the Mediterranean, she studied Italian cooking at Apicius, the International School of Hospitality in Florence, Italy, and continues to explore the culinary traditions of Italy in her travels.

Viktorija is an intrepid culinary explorer who seeks out unique and traditional foods in each area she visits. During her travels in Sardinia, she worked with chefs and home cooks to gather the traditional recipes of this magical island. She gathers those recipes in this cookbook, educating readers not only about Sardinian food but also about Sardinian wine, tradition, and culture.

Viktorija's first cookbook, *The Puglian Cookbook: Bringing the Flavors of Puglia Home*, was published by Surrey Books in April 2011. She is the host and coproducer of the DVD release *Sardinia: Food and Wine*. This entertaining and informative collection of stories and interviews make the island of Sardinia come to life.

Viktorija lives in Chicago, where she teaches cooking and wine classes.

Also by Viktorija Todorovska

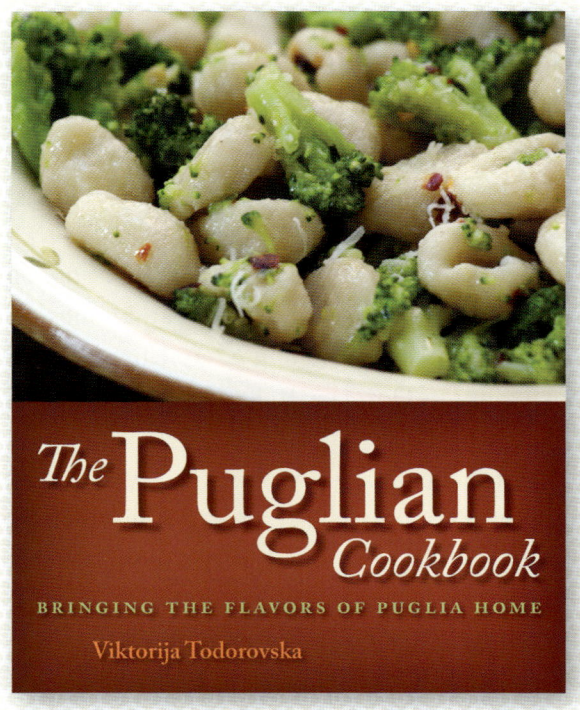

We love that before cranking up the heat at the stove, Todorovska pauses to make sure we have a deep understanding of the ingredients that are the fundamentals of Puglian cuisine. She writes for the home cook, with no fancy tricks, no hard-to-find ingredients. —CHICAGO TRIBUNE

ISBN 978-1-57284-117-8 • $20

AVAILABLE AT BOOKSELLERS EVERYWHERE

AN AGATE IMPRINT